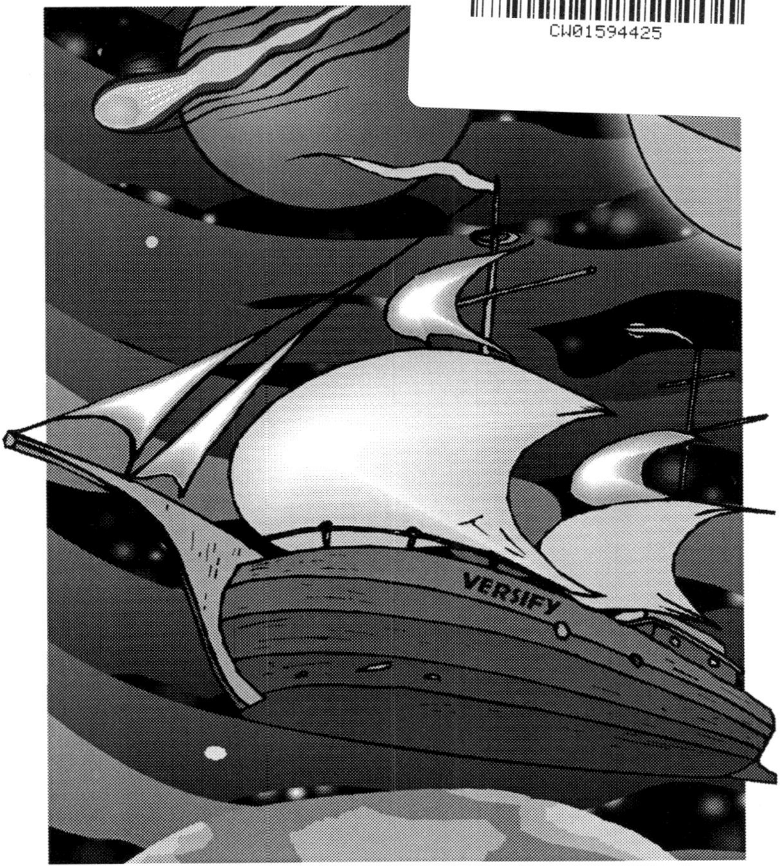

POETIC VOYAGES NORTHAMPTONSHIRE

Edited by Natalie Nightingale

First published in Great Britain in 2001 by
YOUNG WRITERS
Remus House,
Coltsfoot Drive,
Peterborough, PE2 9JX
Telephone (01733) 890066

HB ISBN 1 86161 924 3
SB ISBN 1 86161 929 4

Foreword

Young Writers was established in 1991 with the aim to promote creative writing in children, to make reading and writing poetry fun.

This year once again, proved to be a tremendous success with over 88,000 entries received nationwide.

The Poetic Voyages competition has shown us the high standard of work and effort that children are capable of today. It is a reflection of the teaching skills in schools, the enthusiasm and creativity they have injected into their pupils shines clearly within this anthology.

The task of selecting poems was therefore a difficult one but nevertheless, an enjoyable experience. We hope you are as pleased with the final selection in *Poetic Voyages Northamptonshire* as we are.

CONTENTS

The Poems

BONFIRE NIGHT

Fireworks flying up high into a dark cloudy sky.
Birds are scared stupid so they speedily fly away.
Swirling, whirling, bright fireworks whiz into the sky.
Children happily enjoy colourful, sparkling sparklers
In total darkness.
Bonfires brightly burn
Excitement pours from an amused crowd.
Catherine wheels spin wildly.
Rockets explode in the sky
While children laugh as well as cheer.
Dogs howl, cats wail, while people enjoy themselves.
Returning people eat their burgers.

Kirsty O'Hara (11)
Alfred Street Junior School

WHAT'S WRONG?

What's wrong?
You look upset,
Please don't cry,
Tell my why,
You seem quite bad
And very sad,
Just smile!

Sarah Jayne Bradshaw (10)
Alfred Street Junior School

NOISES

I heard a noise,
Who's there?
What's there?
Shuffle, shuffle,
Who is it?
Is it the headless ghost man?
Phew!
It was only the trees
Swaying in the wind
Like a whirlwind.
'Please stop,'
I say to myself.
I heard a noise.

Leanne Wood (10)
Alfred Street Junior School

MY BUTTERFLY

Yellow dot,
Sunny spot,

Creeping crawler,
Munching cruncher,

Time taking,
Wing making,

That's what makes
My butterfly.

Zoe Horrell (11)
Alfred Street Junior School

LEAVES

Trees blowing,
With the stars in the sky,
I wonder why?
Together both stars and moon glow,
So that I know
It is night-time.

Whistling and howling
In the darkness,
Noises from everywhere,
Mostly animals
That make them.

Branches on trees,
Leaves falling off,
People walk on them,
Cold in the dark,
I feel there's nobody there,
Of course there is,
Help! I'm scared!

Kayleigh Brennan (10)
Alfred Street Junior School

SCARY NIGHT

Lightning clashed against the trees
You heard the sound of moving leaves
I felt a chill across my back
Something was behind me
Was it a monster or an alien?
I turned around
I saw nothing on that scary night.

Rachel Davitte (9)
Alfred Street Junior School

Four Seasons Of The Year

The snow is falling,
Ice is covering the lake,
Ducks can't swim anymore.

The buds are popping,
New greatly coloured flowers,
They brighten the world.

The sun is shining,
Some children are playing out,
They are all shouting.

The leaves are falling,
Dew is covering the grass,
Some dogs are barking.

Kirsty-Louise Green (11) & Karen Simmons (10)
Alfred Street Junior School

Kenning

A yellow dot,
A small tot,

A tiny creature,
With a wriggly feature,

Wait to change,
To rearrange,

Wings emerge,
Skyward surge,

Here am I, butterfly.

Michael Farrow (11)
Alfred Street Junior School

Dear Maureen

Dear Maureen,

I am a bed;
It's not fair, I'm very delicate;
Dark nights,
Warm snug covers,
A pillow heavily on me,
Tossing, turning,
Morning comes, she awakes,
Making breakfast,
She sits on me, cold and wet, milk.

Yours sincerely
Beccie Bedspring

Samantha Keywood (11)
Alfred Street Junior School

A 1964 Dad

1964 Dad.
Loud rear end.
Mouth needs a bend.
Couch potato.
Never misses a football match,
Especially Man United ones.
Always lazy,
Slow thinking,
Needs teaching a lot.
Coming to exchange week;
I think he needs new feet
(What I mean is he doesn't get around much)!

Ashley Redman (11)
Alfred Street Junior School

MYSTERIOUS DARKNESS

Rustling, howling,
Distant traffic,
Shadows leaping,
In the darkness.

I'm alone,
No warmth around,
No heat,
No one to turn to,
Darkness.

Moving lights,
Sparkling flashes,
Could be aliens,
Scary, terrifying.

Shivering, nervous,
Shaking, fear,
Colour changing,
Howling animals,
Darkness.

Muddy wellies,
Muddy clothes,
Water, puddles,
Darkness.

My friends are all around me,
As the strong wind ruffles my hair,
I'm warmer inside than outside
Because my spirit stays hot.

Joanne Peel (10)
Alfred Street Junior School

Spooksville

Ghosts are very scary,
They always make me jump,
I can hear chains rattling,
And my heart goes thump, thump, thump,
Vampires suck your blood,
In the middle of the night,
If you ever saw one,
It would give you such a fright.
Witches fly on brooms,
With a lucky black cat,
Frogs and snails and puppy dog tails,
I don't think you'd like that.
Werewolves howl,
In the middle of the night,
They are very hairy,
It could make your face go white.

I like scary stories,
I hope you do too,
If you're feeling frightened,
I wouldn't look behind you!

Emma Anniwell (9)
Alfred Street Junior School

I've Got . . .

I've got fishes on my fingers,
Tails on my toes,
But now I know
I've got nothing on my nose!

Adina-Leigh Collins (9)
Alfred Street Junior School

Dear Maureen

Dear Maureen

I am a bench;
Almost everyday somebody sits on me,
Sometimes heavy geeks
Sometimes light guys.
There's this man he's really fat
He wears this coat,
It's white and black.
And there's a lady, she's really posh,
I heard somebody say
Her house is full of dosh.
What should I do
I'm bending in the middle,
I'm hurting, help!

Yours bent and broken.
Benji Bench

Emma-Jade Laughton (10)
Alfred Street Junior School

Seasons

Spring again,
Flowers grow.
Summer sun,
Wind blow.
Autumn days,
Leaves of trees.
Wintertime,
Snowflakes fall.

Nadana Papworth (9)
Alfred Street Junior School

TENNIS GAME

This is the tennis racket
That hit the ball.

This is the tennis racket
That hit the ball
That went over the net.

This is the tennis racket
That hit the ball
That went over the net
That got the points.

This is the tennis racket
That hit the ball
That went over the net
That got the points
That hit the man
Now he can't play tennis anymore.

Grant King (9)
Alfred Street Junior School

THE NIGHT

The moon was a glistening light,
Shining through the night.
The water was a trickling flow,
And the wind was not even a blow.

A lot of planes came in the sky,
All went rushing by.
Some stars were twinkling, shining bright
Too blazing to glimpse a sight.

Alexander Toleman-Edwards (9)
Alfred Street Junior School

In The Darkness

It's quite dark where I am,
No light, just noises.
Some colour in the sky,
Black, grey, white and orange,
Flashing through my mind.

Wind whistling through my clothes,
Chilling me to the bone.
I feel like I am lonely,
But there are people all around me.

There's a light in the sky,
Flashing red and white.
What could it be?
Perhaps it is an alien spaceship,
Or maybe just an aeroplane.

It's muddy and wet,
Sploshing in my wellies.
Suddenly a light,
Maybe a shooting star.

Feeling quite scared now,
Animal noises frightening me.
Suddenly silence, all around,
In darkness.

Olivia Guest (9)
Alfred Street Junior School

Looking And Listening

I am walking under the stars,
The traffic is going past,
The clouds pass by the moon,
There are ripples in the water.

I am walking under the moonlight,
The wind is rushing through my hair,
The shadows of lots of people,
There is a glow in the sky.

Nadine Swords (9)
Alfred Street Junior School

THE AUTUMN WEATHER

It's a miserable day
With the wind whipping.
Crispy brown leaves off the tree,
They float to the ground like a
Cradle rocking.
They land on the moistened earth
With their baby friends.
The sun is hibernating,
In its nest of clouds,
Asleep for its long wait till summer,
So it can water over
The children playing and having fun.

Clouds all soft, fluffy, white,
Like untrodden snow.
In the rough, wild, whipping wind
Boys and girls with kites,
Like huge Chinese dragons.
Swirling their tails,
In the air.
Wind is ripping leaves off the tree,
Like scraps of torn paper scattered
All over the floor.
Leaves are brown, yellow, gold,
Crunchy cheese and onion crisps.

Paul Southey (11) & Ryan Kalla (10)
Alfred Street Junior School

THE FOOT

This is the foot
That kicked the ball
Which scored the goal
That won the match
To win the cup
And this is the hand
That saved the goals
Against the opposition.

Mark Pearce (10)
Alfred Street Junior School

THE STORM

Storms are thunder
Storms are lightning
Storms split rocks
Storms are frightening
Clashing thunder
Splashing rain
Sunny weather comes again.

Tony Bright (10)
Alfred Street Junior School

MISERY

I can't go to Everdon,
I'm really upset,
I'd give up anything for it,
Even my best pet!

Shauni Maple (10)
Alfred Street Junior School

Night-Time

The moon is glowing, glowing like a silver ball,
The trees look like they were frozen in time,
The stream trickling,
The stars twinkling in the sky,

The forest, looking like the soul of a sandal,
In the distance the lights of other towns,
The planes floating in the sky,
The headlights of cars blinking between the trees,

The animals making noises,
The sky is all different shades of grey,
The wind is not even blowing,
Me feeling nothing I've felt before.

Aaron Flynn (10)
Alfred Street Junior School

It's Raining

It's raining,
I hate it when it's raining.
It's boring,
Nothing to do.
Just sitting around doing nothing,
Waiting for the rain to stop.
The sun's coming out,
But it's still raining,
The rain is stopping,
Yes!
The rain has stopped,
Now I can go out to play.

Lee Kane (10)
Alfred Street Junior School

THE FEELING OF BEING LONELY IN DARKNESS

I'm lonely,
My family aren't around,
The gentle wind is the only sound,
The moon shines down with hopeful light,
To cheer me up all through the night,
The chilly air collides with the breeze,
Swaying swiftly, blow the trees,
Animals bleat from far away,
If they stay up late it's sleep for the day,
I'm lonely, I feel wiggly and jiggly inside,
I'm scared and nervous I've just got to hide,
My friends act as if I'm not there,
I'm too lonely and they just stare,
The feeling of being in the night,
Is calm, steady, perfectly right!

Charlotte Hewitt (9)
Alfred Street Junior School

SWAP A BROTHER

1993 Brother.
Good at annoying people.
Needs a good telling off
every now and then
to keep him in place.
Runs on vegetables.
Keep him away from kitchen tables
and especially wire cables.
He will be lots of fun
but you must take him for a run.
We will swap for anything but a dog.

Emily Crump (11)
Alfred Street Junior School

Night Walk

It was a cold, dark, soundless night,
The gentle wind rustled through the trees
Which were like dark silhouettes
Standing out on the horizon.
The moon, one stage from being full,
Stood out in the sky
Like the sun giving us all light.
We walked along the footpath,
The gentle padding of our wellies shattering the silence.
We stop. What was that?
We stand there shivering in our wellies.
Ahh well, we move on and finish our night walk.

Christopher Dominy (10)
Alfred Street Junior School

A Tiny Dot

A tiny dot,
A brewing pot.

A little wriggler,
A moving squiggler.

A silky bed,
'I'm new,' he said.

A winged beauty,
A flying cutie.

I'm a butterfly!

James Banyard (11)
Alfred Street Junior School

Why

Why do I have to go to bed?
Why can't I stay up a bit later?
Why doesn't the dog use a knife and fork?
Why can't you answer my questions Dad?

Why is the sofa pink?
Why are your shoes red?
Why are you wearing a tie?
Stop saying why.
Why?

Andrew Constant (10)
Alfred Street Junior School

What Do Teachers Do When They Get Home?

Do they fiddle about?
Or go to sleep?
Do they wear bright red dressing gowns?
Or do they slurp their soup?
Do they watch the Diamonds score 2-0?
Or do they drink gin?
The next day they feel dim.

Timothy Bei (9)
Alfred Street Junior School

The Glistening Night

The moon was as still as a statue,
It was a glistening ball that hovered in the sky,
The sky was a dull grey and orange
And it caught my eye.

The planes that were in the sky,
Just went by,
The planes looked small,
But they were not small, they were big.

Dean Bareford (9)
Alfred Street Junior School

I'M DAY DREAMING

Mum thinks I'm listening,
But I'm flying through the air like a feather . . .
Me and Ben (From A1) are on the beach together.

Dad thinks I'm tidying my room,
But I'm talking to Nadana . . .
I'm eating a big banana.

Karena thinks I'm writing,
But I'm sitting on cloud nine . . .
I'm drinking some wine.

Terry thinks I'm singing,
But I'm having a make-over . . .
I'm running to Dover.

Soraya Pearce (10)
Alfred Street Junior School

WIND

Wind is like a tantrum just about to start,
Indoors we stay away from the cold,
Never go out in the blistering wind
'Cos doors rattle while the wind blows.

Charlotte Dickinson (10)
Braunston CE Primary School

TREASURE HUNT

T is for *treasure* you're hoping to find.
R is for *ravenous* that you feel in your mind.
E is for *ever* and *ever* for the time when you search.
A is for *animal,* a parrot in fact that sits on its perch.
S is for *savages* that you might have to fight.
U is for *under* the stars where you'd sleep at night.
R is for *rubies* that would be in the treasure chest.
E is for *ever* after that always looks best.

H is for *hunt* that takes you forever.
U is for *understanding* and sticking together.
N is for *noises* that come from all around.
T is for *treasure* which is now finally found.

Rachel Hall (9)
Braunston CE Primary School

SUPER MUM

Super mum, you're wonderful,
you cook, clean and wash.

Super mum, you're wonderful,
you buy clothes, toys and books.

Super mum, you're wonderful,
you let me go riding, swimming and singing.

Super mum, you're wonderful
and that's the way I like you!

Jocelyn Gilbert (10)
Braunston CE Primary School

It's Raining Again

It's raining again
It's raining night and day
It's flooding the fields, roads and houses
Oh what a pain.

It's raining again
The people are saying this is nature at its worst
The people are saying this is natural, oh what a curse
The people are leaving their homes in their hundreds
It's raining again.

The world's climate is playing a game
The weather is heading for a disaster
The people are saying that we are to blame
It's raining again.

The ozone is getting worse
The cause is all that gas
All the cars always come first
Maybe the people are right
We are the masters of disasters
It's raining again.

Korin Cotton (10)
Braunston CE Primary School

My Bird Of Prey

I once had a bird of prey,
He ate chicks every day.
One day he died,
But, he is still alive
In my heart in every way.

Tristan Bell (10)
Braunston CE Primary School

TWISTER

Twister, twister,
Do you want more,
You get something stronger,
When you come for advice,
Wind and storms applied.

Typhoon, typhoon,
I know you want more,
I'll give you something windier,
When you come and ask me,
Tornadoes and hurricanes at the ready.

Tornado, tornado,
We think you want more,
You get something bigger,
When you remove my door,
Earthquakes are more advanced.

Andrew Lord (10)
Braunston CE Primary School

WINTER

W inter is cold, winter is wet
I n the snow children play
N ear houses children make snowmen
T o wish the snow would stay forever and ever
E very child in the close is throwing snowballs
at their own home
R emember the days of winter.

Luke Cawthorne (10)
Braunston CE Primary School

My Cat

My cat Gnasher
He's a real smasher.
He's ginger and white
Like carrots and mash.
He loves a belly rub
And a good back scratch.
He's fat and furry.
He sleeps like a baby
And plays like a monkey.
His purr is as loud as a lion's roar
But his meow is squeaky like a little mouse
Especially when his food is about.
I love my cat Gnasher
He is my best friend.

Dean Williams (10)
Braunston CE Primary School

Laces

Laces are long,
Laces are strong,
You tie them up
Then you go wrong.

Laces are thick,
Laces are thin,
They go round and round
Then they go in.

Laces, laces, I hate laces,
Mum said I do it at fast paces.

Rajen Mistry (9)
Braunston CE Primary School

My Hamster

My hamster is a pain
He bangs on his cage again and again.
He chewed my curtains into tiny bits
He bit my sister and she said that was it
Mum said, 'He must go!'
Dad and me said, 'No, no, no!'
I love my hamster
I couldn't bear it if he left
Even though sometimes he is a pest.

Gwendoline Ford (10)
Braunston CE Primary School

What Is The Sun?

Is the sun a basketball in the sky?
Is the sun a golden top from a milk bottle?
Is the sun a beach ball that's been kicked into the sky?
Is the sun a gold coin on the ground?
Is the sun a massive fireball?
Is the sun a sparkling sphere?
Is the sun a unique star?
What do you think the sun is?

Louise Williams (9)
Braunston CE Primary School

Dogs Sleep Anywhere

Dogs sleep anywhere
On a floor, on a chair,
Dogs sleep anywhere
They don't care.

Dogs sleep anywhere
My mum said,
Dogs sleep anywhere
But mostly on my bed.

Jade Simpson (10)
Braunston CE Primary School

WHAT'S IN THE BOX?

A magic lamp to let the genie sleep.
A golden goose to make me money.
An imaginary friend to help the lonely.
A star to finish the constellation.
A door to enter the other mystical world.
A green pane of glass to finish the palace.
A new recipe for that sweet inventor.
A hoot of an owl to warn the mouse.
A golden boot to reward the footballing star.
A golden medal to reward the heroes.

Luke Ogden (10)
Hazel Leys Primary School

WHAT'S IN THE BOX?

A bit of red to complete the unfinished rainbow.
A Mr Scott to begin the lesson right on time.
A bit of egg for he who fell off the wall.
A 'she' for a 'he' who wanted love.
A bucket of water for those little children.
A 'y' for the end of Tracy.

Nikki Fraser (11)
Hazel Leys Primary School

WHAT'S IN THE BOX?

A magic pair of slippers to make you dance forever.
A bit of everything you want.
A dream for when you sleep at night.
A friend for when you're lonely.
A ray of sunlight to warm up the day.
A day to complete one whole week.
A cloud to float up in the sky.
A key to open the locked door.
A gobstopper to suck to the end of time.
A bag of forgets for someone to remember.

Barry Hunter (11)
Hazel Leys Primary School

WHAT'S IN THE BOX?

A pink ticket to collect my winnings.
A goose to lay the golden egg.
A key to open the mysterious door.
A magic medicine to make me better.
An apple that falls off the tree.
A pen so I can write stories.
A book to make the day shorter.
A woolly jumper to keep me cosy.
A secret to share with my friend.
A grinning hyena to make me laugh.

Kerry Streatfield (11)
Hazel Leys Primary School

What's In The Box?

Two turtle doves for the second day.
A star for the three men to follow.
A magic lamp to get three wishes.
A watch to stop the hands of time.
A bit of memory for the year 1945.
A magic key for Alice to open the door.
A carrot for a peckish rabbit.
A ring of a bell to start a fresh school day.
A place to explore the lands and oceans.
A shiny medal for the brave.

David Clark (10)
Hazel Leys Primary School

What's In The Box?

A golden egg to give to a hen,
A coin to fill my money box,
A star that came out in Bethlehem,
A spell for three witches to read,
A time warp to go back in history,
An adventure for a dog to complete,
A fossil to be discovered,
A whistle for the birds to sing,
A lamp for a genie to live in,
Another box to keep you going.

Lauren Wilson (9)
Hazel Leys Primary School

What's In The Box

A gobstopper for that everlasting taste.
A wishing machine for my third and final wish.
A bright star for that everlasting twinkle.
A fossil from another amazing creature.
A bit of luck to win a competition.
A spell so my troubles go away.
A golden egg so my dream will come true.
A watch with that extra hour.
A lamp to get me out of trouble.
A golden feather that has drifted from a creature.

Lee McNamee (11)
Hazel Leys Primary School

What's In The Box?

A bag of forgets for someone to remember.
A mystical land waiting to be explored.
A door which leads to another adventure.
A delightful memory which has been forgotten.
A crystal ball which beholds the future.
A tasty gobstopper waiting to be sucked.
A silent secret which should never be told.
A wishing machine for my third and final wish.
A shiny gold egg laid by the golden goose.
A star to lead us to new-born life.

Rachel Croft (11)
Hazel Leys Primary School

WHAT'S IN THE BOX?

A magic lamp to reveal another's destiny.
A bag of forgets for someone with no memory.
A door to the mind to explore the brain.
A book to take me into a great adventure.
A golden egg to foresee the future.
A magic wand for my third and final wish.
A magnificent memory to remember always.
A star to add to the great one's belt.
A faint whisper never to be heard.
A golden feather plucked from a golden eagle.

Ashleigh Middleton (11)
Hazel Leys Primary School

WHAT'S IN THE BOX

A book for a witch's spell.
A star for the three men to follow.
A lamp for that boy.
A bit of luck to win a competition.
A golden goose that belongs to the queen.
A door for all your troubles.
A gobstopper with that never-ending taste.
A fossil belonging to an archaeologist.
A bag of money to pay your bills.
A spell for a wizard's potion.

Ryan Williamson (11)
Hazel Leys Primary School

What's In The Box?

A glowing star to join the other millions,
A time warp to go to the Victorian times to revise,
A magic piece of paper to write this for you, to read this today,
A magic lamp to wish with, for my last and final wish,
Another world to see the contents within its space,
A fossil worth millions to give the museum,
A tiptoe as I sneak out at night to come and play,
A never-ending bouncing ball to bounce all day,
A ripped page to finish off to send to you,
Another empty box to be recycled to help you.

Sarah-Jane Spence (10)
Hazel Leys Primary School

What's In The Box?

Nothing, to add to that nothingness in the world.
Anything, for anything else.
A star, to lead us back to our shelter.
A magic land, for that other place.
A magic lamp, for the genie's own home.
A magic carpet, to take us back home.
A bag of forgets, for a forgetful person.
A spell, to cook a perfect meal.
A wand, to entertain us all, good.
A time warp, to see another dimension.

Michael Thomas (10)
Hazel Leys Primary School

What's In The Box

A book full of magic that could be all mine.
A beautiful island I can relax on all day and all night long.
A chocolate factory for when I arrive back home.
A flying carpet to explore the world.
A lovely memory to share to myself.
A secret I can share with my best friend.
A laugh for everyone who's in the class.
A fossil to discover the ancient old world.
A bit of everything you wanted.
A magical washing machine to end my poem.

Michaela McCabe (11)
Hazel Leys Primary School

What's In The Box?

A golden key to open a door
A gingerbread man to fill my tummy
A mini TV to keep me entertained
A chiming clock to tell me the time
A supernatural colour to complete my picture
A magical star to tell me the way
A wishing well to give me a wish
A fortune teller to answer my problems
A funny clown to make me chuckle
A sparkling crystal to finish my necklace.

Sarah Finlay (10)
Hazel Leys Primary School

What's In The Box?

A whirling door to another dimension.
A piece of treasure for my collection.
A star to guide you along.
A bark from the dog next door.
A coin scratch from a winning card.
An old fossil from prehistoric life.
An egg to fall off a wall.
A lamp for me to gently rub.
A boat for me to sail on.
A seed for me to plant.

Andrew Blackwood (10)
Hazel Leys Primary School

What's In The Box?

A genie to go with my magic lamp.
A new world to make, start over.
A goose that laid a golden egg.
A star that twinkles all night long.
A fossil that twinkles and marks a creature
under the world.
A slipper that doesn't fit the Ugly Sisters.
An 'X' that marks the spot.

Jack Blakeston (11)
Hazel Leys Primary School

A Snail's Journey

I am a snail.
My journey is not far,
But it is hard to get past the car.
I am slow, when I am on the go,
I am not fast like a dog,
Nor can I hop like a frog,
But I can travel, please don't laugh
My journey is so hard.
I could get crushed or eaten.
I'm not boasting but I may be
    the bravest animal alive,
Even though I find it hard to survive
It's still my travel.

Charlie Whitham (11)
Henry Gotch Junior School

I'm In A Car!

I'm in a car,
Travelling far,
Far, far away,
But when I got there the beach was bare
Because everybody was at the fair.
We went on the rides and the slides,
After I did that I won a bat,
After that, I was so hot
So I went to a shop.
I went to a shop for my sister Molly,
To get a lolly.

Vicky McAlwane (10)
Henry Gotch Junior School

The Solar System Tour

Climb aboard! Climb aboard!
You'll love the tour.
We know, we know you will!
You'll have a lifetime's thrill!

You'll spot six million stars!
See Venus. See Neptune.
We'll whiz you right round Saturn
Then Mercury onto Mars.

Don't forget Jupiter and Uranus!
Pluto as well! Earth and Mars!
So, climb aboard on the spaceship!
Be quick! We're leaving soon!

Natasha Bains (11)
Henry Gotch Junior School

Journey

I went on a walk
Grass like blunt needles.

I went on a car journey
Traffic like mad ants.

I went on a steam train
As slow as a snail.

I went on a ship
As rough as a rollercoaster.

I went in a rocket
As fast as a cheetah.

Jason Franks (11)
Henry Gotch Junior School

Our Vehicles

We're in the car
We've gone afar.

We're in a balloon
We look like a baboon.

We're on a plane
We have no fame.

We're on a train
We will never do it again.

We're on a ferry
We are even very merry.

We're on a bus
We make a fuss.

We're very tired
We both got *fired*!

Carrie Spencer (10)
Henry Gotch Junior School

Plane Abduction

On the plane,
Came a light.
On my journey,
Came a light.
I could not see,
I felt cold,
I felt a sting.
I opened my eyes,
I was home . . .

Connor Tate (10)
Henry Gotch Junior School

UP AND AWAY

Ready for take off!
Let's go!
Up and away!
Our journey goes faraway from today,
Look up at the candyfloss clouds,
Oh no, here comes the hail and rain,
Maybe there will be a blizzard or even a hurricane!
Up and away!
Possibly our lives could end today!
C S
R M
A A
S S
H H
! !

This is where it breaks off!

Jessica Bhangal (11)
Henry Gotch Junior School

THE GHOST FROM MUMBLING HILL

They rumble and stumble
And never keep still
They chat and row,
They look and look,
They bellow and shout,
They never stop still . . .
Waiting for a ghost all night,
What a really bad fright!

Robbie Kennedy (10)
Henry Gotch Junior School

TORNADO

Round and round it goes,
Who knows where it's going to stop,

It carries on from now to when,
Until it stops,

Twirling, swirling, frantically turning,
Until it stops,

No one knows why it spins,
Maybe it's angry, maybe it grins.

Round and round it goes,
Who knows where it's going to stop.

Anthony Newton (11)
Henry Gotch Junior School

THE JOURNEY TO THE SHOP

I went to the shop
On a stormy day
When the thunder clashed
Like an elephant screaming
and stamping away.

I ran in the shop
As fast as a cheetah
I brought an umbrella
And went home dry but cold.

Leanne Tate (10)
Henry Gotch Junior School

I Would Love To Go To The Moon

I would love to go to the moon
And I would love to go soon.
To float in space and feel so free,
To have somewhere with no gravity.
I could pretend I was a fish,
Oh, going to the moon would be my wish,
Just to swim in the air,
But there is one thing I can not bear!
The journey home and the journey there!

Jessica Berwick (10)
Henry Gotch Junior School

Holiday Journey

I am in the car on the way to the sea
The journey is so long and slow
Then we get out and walk on the beach
And a crab bit my dad's toe.

Out comes the sun
So lovely and hot
I ask my dad if his toe is all right
He said, 'No, it is not!'

Charlotte Panther (10)
Henry Gotch Junior School

A Long Journey To The Moon

I'm going to the moon
With a big balloon.
I'm going all the way up
In a big great cup.
I brought some money
I wish it was sunny!
I am so sleepy
But the darkness is creepy.
I'll be safely there soon
On the magical moon.

Manpreet Shergill (10)
Henry Gotch Junior School

Travelling

I'm in the car
Travelling far,
The sun is out
And I'm burning hot.

I'm at the seaside at last,
The car wasn't going fast,
I went to get an ice lolly,
Boy, am I jolly.

Bryony Barritt (10)
Henry Gotch Junior School

James Slob

James is such a slob,
Unlike the rest of the street.
He is worse than a blob,
But he eats many a sweet.

The sweety's name is Galaxy,
The commanding officer of space.
The other sweet is called Twixi,
Who likes to have a race.

James imagines Twixi,
Running round a track.
Doing thirty laps of tricks,
Until his face turns black.

Galaxy is in his spaceship,
Fighting evil aliens.
But the fish is ended in a rip,
As James just dazes 'im.

So James has an imagination,
Or so he says to the entire nation.

Darren Blakeley (11)
Irchester Junior School

The Sleeping Lion

I am a lonely lion,
Prancing through the jungle,
With my golden roar,
I frighten Zippy, George and Bungle.

I chase mice just for fun,
But sometimes they turn then I run and run,
But after all it is still fun,
All I want, is a chum.

When I go to the pack,
They send me to go out the back,
When I go out the back,
I always seem to go back.

I tell my parents of these dreams,
But they don't know what I mean,
When I go to sleep,
The dreams start to repeat.

Jake Sanders (10)
Irchester Junior School

My Magical Bed

I sleep in my bed,
And lay my head.
When I dream there is a magical land.
With my favourite pop band.

'Get out from under there,' says my mother
'And get back in your cover.'

My bed is wonderful,
It is so colourful,
Everyone thinks I am dumb
Especially my mum.

My bed is a car,
It goes very far.
It is a plane,
But that is too plain.

I can't wait to go to sleep,
In my bed that wasn't cheap.

Chloe Arrowsmith (11)
Irchester Junior School

WALKING BACK FROM SCHOOL

I was walking back from school
On a Friday eve.
But then I saw a fly
Flying overhead,
But no, it is a hawk,
A flock of hawks I see
Fighting with the bee.
They caught the bee
And flew back home
With their scrumptious tea.

I carried on my walking
I was going to be late for tea
From around the corner
A dog came to see
But no, it is a lion,
Not a lion in the street
This really could not be.
Suddenly I realised
The trees were all around me.

I began to shout
I ran and ran
And then I fell
Unconscious I lay,
My thoughts were unknown
For all eternity
They will never be discovered
Only between you and me.

Tom George (11)
Irchester Junior School

THE TWIST

Half the class are up and down,
While the other half just sit around.
They never learn, they just sit and stare
The other half never frown, they get everything right,
And never have to care.

But one day, it turned around
It all went up the stairs;
Nobody listened they all just stared
Day-dreamed of the fair.
They invented rides long and fair
And even wearing underwear.

While the other half were getting it right 2+2 and 9 x that,
The teacher was puzzled,
'I don't understand what happened to the kids.'
'But maybe I'll treat them to a bag of sweets!'

Charlotte Inglesant (11)
Irchester Junior School

DREAM LAND

I started to lay my head down,
For a wonderful fantasy dream.
I thought about what dream I'd have,
Or whether I'd have one at all!

What would it be, I cannot wait,
Oh please be quiet, brother mate!
What will it be?
You will have to wait and see!

Lauren Rawlings (10)
Irchester Junior School

A Fantasy Dream

I was asleep in a dream
Dreaming about a merry-go-round
I was spinning and spinning
Not once did my feet touch the ground

Then I was on a rollercoaster
Up and down, up and down
Around and around
Like a poster.

It was great at the fair
With candy
And with sweets
But sadly I have to end my dream
With a goodnight's sleep
Fair! Fair! Fair!

Kimberley Hinde (10)
Irchester Junior School

Mum, Can I . . .

'Mum, I'm tired, can I go to bed?'
'Of course you can dear, you sleepy head.'

'Mum can I get a drink? I'm very thirsty you see.'
'Of course you can dear, how about a can of beer.'

'Mum can I have something to eat?
I'm very hungry you see.'
'No, you cannot, now go to bed,
If I hear you come down those stairs one more time
You will be sleeping in the shed!'

Kylie Abrahams (11)
Irchester Junior School

I Was Visited By Aliens

Last night I was visited by aliens,
It was quite a scare at first
They said they are real people but had been cursed,
One had red googly eyes
Another had fingers shaped like apple pies,
But they were both really nice guys.

Their spaceship was really cool,
They even had a swimming pool,
Clang, who ponged a bit
Showed me around the ship.
I fell down a huge deep dip,
Clang got me out, I felt sick.

I wanted to go home,
After I had seen their big dome
They said to me, 'Do you like cream?'
I woke up it was just a dream!

Laura Jolley (10)
Irchester Junior School

Bed Brawl

I lay awake in my bed,
With my covers over my head.
Army men fight for their lives,
One fell, in the bin he lies.

In the darkness they fight away,
I'm now in bed, they're tucked away.
Now I have to go to sleep,
I think I'll see them again next week.

Brent Leighton (11)
Irchester Junior School

My Fantasy Land

In my fantasy land
Are ice creams all around,
I can drink cocoa
And eat Polos
Under my fluffy duvet cover.

I can pretend I'm in the jungle,
Climbing up and down,
Or pretend I'm on a roundabout,
Going round and round.

But when it is morning,
It really is boring,
I like my land,
My very own fantasy land.

Rachel Hancock (10)
Irchester Junior School

Battle In My Bed

I make a battlefield in my bed
Climbing, falling off my head.
They're battling hard and make a boom
And it ends up like a battle dome.

The vehicles fall off and down
Then end up in my dressing gown.
Behind my pillows that's where they hide
Battling away, but most of them died.

A final battle of a few,
The soldiers end up old not new,
Now the battle has come to an end
I will play with them until they break and bend.

Paul Porter (11)
Irchester Junior School

I Am

Lots think I'm a day dreamer
But really I'm not
I am quite weird
And sometimes lose the plot

I do my best at school work
And try very hard
But when I go in pubs
I always get barred.

I think about my future
What could I do?
I could be a vet
So could you too.

I am very strange
And a bit dumb,
But when I get scared
I always find my mum.

I don't want to hurt anyone
I only want to be
A very pleasant boy
A part of class three.

Danielle Morgan (11)
Irchester Junior School

THE DEN OF MY DREAMS

I pull over my feather duvet.
Night is falling,
Close those eyes, close those eyes.
The town lights go to sleep,
Everything in deep sleep.

I'm dreaming of a fallen willow tree,
Its long green hair swinging in the breeze,
A rusty trickle of water it makes
Nettles surround its queen, as the willow awaits
The nettles sway, get ready for a sting.

I awoke, in the light of the morning
Silence, silence, nothing is to be heard,
Only the noise of people in deep sleep.
Go back to my dream, but
No, it's passed away into the wilderness.

Rachel Painter (10)
Irchester Junior School

SEALIFE IN MAY

In the morning,
The sea awakes,
Sealife arises,
Dolphins make mates.

Whales are pouncing,
As fish swim away.
Sea turtles are creeping
In the month of May.

Sea horses are galloping,
Through the weeds,
As fishermen catch
The fish of the sea.

Seagulls are waiting,
For the feast of the day,
As it all is happening
In the month of May.

Rachel Layram (10)
Irchester Junior School

The Sweety Tea

Yesterday, I think it was,
Though they're all the same,
Some think that when it rains it's really such a shame,
But I don't!
As I go out in the streets
I cannot resist to stick out my tongue
And have a sweety tea,
There's so many to choose from, you just come and see!
There's liquorice and candied fruit, what a sight to see!
There's runny toffee and bubblegum,
Come on now, let's have some fun and you will see . . .

Yum, yum, yum,
A sweety tea, but mum gets angry, yes indeed,
Oh dear, oh dear I'm glad I had a sweety tea,
I would be so very hungry,
Mum says, I'm very silly putting dirty rain in my tummy.

Hannah Larkman (11)
Irchester Junior School

Colour Of Life

I'm not very bright
In reading or writing.
But the colour of life
Is the life for me.
'Cause everything's multi-coloured
In all that I see,
The colour of life
Is the life for me.

I have dreams of colour
Surrounding a colour,
Bright colour everywhere.
I enjoy seeing colour,
Instead of black and white.
I love the colours of the world
The colour of life,
Is the life for me.

The colour of life,
Is the life for me,
'Cause it wouldn't be
Great if all black and white.
I love colour,
Yes, I do,
The colour of life
Is the life for me.

Adam Tee (11)
Irchester Junior School

The Real World

At school I am very silly,
I hide under the desk and quiver,
The teacher says, 'You are so silly Billy,'
And sometimes I'm a real fibber.
I have a friend called Lauren-Kay
And all she says is, 'You are thick.'
I always go to pack,
But it always makes me feel sick.

At home I'm in the real world
I fight the lion in my room,
But sometimes up I curl
And hide from the big boom!
There's a llama in my room,
Boo, it's gone!
That llama was so easy to scare
All you need is a bon-bon,
But nobody gives a real care,
In my real world I fight lions,
In my real world I kill llamas.

I love the real world,
It's much better than the old one,
Boom! I'm back in the old one,
Back in school, a real bore,
Can't do nothing, still I am silly.

Cheryl Quelch (11)
Irchester Junior School

PETS AND ME!

I have two dogs,
Two ferrets and
Two birds.
The dogs play
With logs,
The ferrets like to
Get merits,
(For what they do),
The birds like to chew,
(On food like Grand New),
That's bird seed, it tastes like goo!
My pets are mad,
They run around so glad . . .
But then there's me, all fine and grand
Walking like I own the land.
But when I eat,
I'm not all grand,
I'm just myself,
And realise I don't own the land!

Andrew Scott (10)
Irchester Junior School

NORMAL FIRST, THEN A STAR

I am a normal cat,
When my owner is around.
But when she goes to school
I am so profound.

I go and visit my girlfriend,
And play with her all day.
Then I get a kipper
Whilst playing with some clay.

Then I go on 'Cats in their Eyes',
I'm Salem, Sabrina's cat.
I talk and talk and do my thing,
Then visit my flat.

By the time my owner's back
I'm asleep on the settee.
The only problem is
She's bought a new cat, Betty!

Hannah Haigh (10)
Irchester Junior School

OH DEAR MY DARLING

Oh dear my darling,
You're so sweet and kind,
Every time I see you
I want to kiss and cuddle you all night.

Oh dear my darling,
You're so sweet and kind,
I love you till the day dawns,
And until the day we die.

Oh dear my darling,
You're so sweet and kind,
I loved you from youth,
And I've come back for you tonight.

Oh dear my darling,
You're so sweet and kind,
I'm very sorry to say this,
But I've got to say bye bye.

Kevin Storke (11)
Irchester Junior School

THE LAND OF DREAMS

I don't know why,
But I have dreams,
Of all different things.
Jungles and balls,
And castle halls,
But it's all just dreams.

A long time ago,
I went to a castle,
Quite a way from here.
There were princesses and dragons
And knights in armour,
But it was just a dream.

One day I went to a fabulous ball,
There was glitter and glam,
But I wasn't that.
I enjoyed dancing, dancing, dancing,
But it was just a dream.
Why can't dreams come true?

Siân-Louise Hill (10)
Irchester Junior School

THE IMAGINATION OF A FRIEND

I have a friend
And she lives up there, (where?)
Up there you know;
Your imagination

She's tall and thin
And has long blonde hair,
But the best thing is . . .
Her ideas

Her ideas are big and bright and great,
Just like her I guess.
We're jungle trekkers in the forest
And police officers who arrest.

We're mermaids swimming up and down,
We're jet bombers bombing to the ground
We're military soldiers, dance all day
And then we go to bed (I pray).

Jade Mortimer (10)
Irchester Junior School

The Animal Of My Dreams

One day, I know, I will have
A hamster, small and fat.
He will run around all night,
And sleep most of the day.

He will be ginger and blonde,
With a small pink nose
And little blue eyes
With a white patch on one.

Toffee, Toffee will be his name,
Because he is so sweet.
His little pink nose will twitch
He loves playing on the football pitch.

This little hamster, Toffee,
Is not a quitter,
He will play and play,
Until he's sweeter than ever before.

Katie Coleman (11)
Irchester Junior School

DREAMY BEAMY

I sit, I lay, I wonder why,
That in my head, I have this spy.

A spy that runs around the town,
A spy that runs up and down.

He runs to south, to east, to west,
Never north, south's his best.

Never had a girlfriend, no one fancies him,
But I'm not surprised, he is rather dim.

He crosses fields, lakes, the sea,
But never ever has he seen me.

But when I wake, it's just a dream,
But he really is my home team.

Lauren Gray (10)
Irchester Junior School

COUCH POTATO

There he is, the couch potato,
With my brother Sctilly Dato
There they lie, hairy and smelly
Just like the button on my big brother's belly
There is just always competition
To watch the television
Couch potato's always there
But Sctilly will always squish him
There's only room for one of them
In the sofa town
So Sctilly decides to eat him
Crunch, crunch and Burrrgh!

Stephen Holloway (11)
Irchester Junior School

JUST STOP AND STARE

When I was at home sitting on the chair,
My sister said, 'Just stop and stare,'
I said, 'Why, what's over there,'
She said, 'Look you see that bear, it is very rare.'

The bear was coming towards us,
Then my mum came running in,
'Oh mum,' we said together, 'you frightened our bear,'
'What bear?' our mother said.

'Oh, you didn't see our bear,
It was over there it looked so kind and gentle,'
'Didn't it,' we said to my guinea pig,
My mum said, 'We have no time to stop and stare.'

Lorna Parker (10)
Irchester Junior School

DINOSAUR BUSH

I watch a human cut some bushes,
Waiting for my big fright
He pulls and pushes,
He is not so bright.

I can feel my legs go numb,
I realise it's him,
He looks so glam,
I think he's had jam.

My waist and down has gone,
My body is next to be done,
It will be my head next,
Then I'll be a small T-rex.

Brodie Lewis (10)
Irchester Junior School

My Dream

I wish, I think, I stare around,
I can't see underground,
And what I see in my heart
I imagine far in my dream.

I wish, I think, I stare around,
I love my dreams, I hate the real world,
We have no time to stand and stare
Beneath the bows.

I wish, I think I stare around,
It says in my dream
I hate and cry
Because of this horrible world.

Jenelle Lambrick (10)
Irchester Junior School

A Small Animal

A small swimmer,
A fast runner.

A brilliant clinger,
A little peeper.

A small creature,
A fast runner.

A good smeller,
A good teller

And that means a kitten.

Finlay Hackett (7)
John Hellins Primary School

A Slimy Belly

A water swimmer
A slimy belly

A little tail
A little tongue

A big mumma
A bigger dad

A little eye
A bigger tongue

Have you guessed it . . .
It's a snake!

Charlotte Emptage (8)
John Hellins Primary School

A Slowcoach

A steady trailer,
A long-eyed head.

A shell hider,
A breakable animal.

A dirty fellow,
A cracky shell.

A slimy . . . *snail*!

Dean Kelly (8)
John Hellins Primary School

School's Out

Hurrah, school's out,
Hurrah, no more school today,
Hurrah, I can go home,
Hurrah, home time, bye-bye stupid
School!

Oh no, more school,
Oh no, back to school,
Oh no, wake up early,
Oh no, car, quick hello horrid
School!

Wuhoo, lunchtime,
Wuhoo, break from work,
Wuhoo, no horrid teacher,
Wuhoo, I can talk to my friends,
Hello lovely *food*!

Hurrah, school's out,
Hurrah, no more school today,
Hurrah, I can go home,
Hurrah, home time, bye-bye stupid
School!

Jayke Annan (8)
John Hellins Primary School

Surprise

A carpet scratcher
A kitchen howler

A smelly surprise
An outside barker

A pencil chewer
A trouser biter

A grey surprise
It makes me a . . . dog!

William Hebblewhite (7)
John Hellins Primary School

A LICKER LICKER

A face licker
A bone chewer

A trouser biter
A furry cuddler

A bone licker

It makes me a . . . puppy!

Megan Ackerley (7)
John Hellins Primary School

THE LITTLE PUPPY

On Monday I got a puppy
On Tuesday I took him for a walk
On Wednesday he followed me to football
On Thursday he played tennis
On Friday he played football
On Saturday he came to school
On Sunday he ate my tea
Oh how cute is he.

Jamie Liptrot (6)
John Hellins Primary School

A Wheel Turner

A small runner
A cute cuddler

A newspaper eater
A wheel turner

A cage player
A furry furball

A cute critter
A fast runner

A good escaper
A good pet

A good friend
A sleeping snorer

A good drinker
A good eater.

You guessed!
A hamster!

Nathan Short (7)
John Hellins Primary School

Summer Day

One day I went to the shop
One day I played
One day I stayed in bed
One day I drove my scooter
One day I went to school
One day it was cool.

Jack Pacey (6)
John Hellins Primary School

I Like Cats

On Monday I went out with cats,
On Tuesday they cried,
On Wednesday we played catch,
On Friday I went out to play,
    not with cats, with rats.
At first they scratched, then they bit.
On Monday I went out,
    not to play but to school,
I chatted to my friends,
I went to school, it was really cool.

Taylor Atkins (7)
John Hellins Primary School

The Strange Pancake

Usually pancakes are more than just flat,
But this one isn't at all that small,
For it was the size of a chair leg on Monday,
It was the size of a car wheel on Tuesday,
It was the size of a door on Wednesday,
It was the size of a house on Thursday,
It was the size of a skyscraper on Friday,
It was soon big enough for the whole world
                    to eat on Sunday!

Shane Kelly (8)
John Hellins Primary School

Lauren And Vaishali

I sit next to the two noisiest people in the class.
This is what they say;
'Give me back my rubber.'
'It's not yours, it's mine.'
'Where have you put my pencil case.'
'Look, is that it flying in the sky.'
'Where?'
'Ha, ha, ha.'
'Look, there it is in front of you.'
'You've been looking in space.'
And I say politely,
'Please be quiet.'
'Yeh Vaishali.'
'Not me Lauren, you.'
And I say,
'Miss, can I move.'

Nikki Hayes (9)
Park Junior School

There Goes Our Teacher

There goes our teacher
Looking like a feature,
Walking through the hall,
She's not very tall,
She's got a long nose,
As long as a hose,
She's got big ears,
We need some shears
And that's our teacher!

Alex Abbotts (10)
Park Junior School

My Day

At the quiet crack of dawn
I got up and had a wash,
I heard my father mowing the lawn
And my mother is very posh.

When I was cleaned up and pretty
We went to the park and built an ark,
I have a cat called Kitty
And my dad's name is Mark

We played at the theme park
And cut my cake in half,
We played and played until it was dark
And went and had our bath.

Grace Simmons (8)
Park Junior School

One Child

One child weak,
One child strong,
One child speaks,
One child longs.

One child jumped,
One child not,
One child remembered
But the other was hot.

One child lies,
One child dies,
One child laughs
And one child cries.

Joanne Monah (8)
Park Junior School

Limerick

There was an old lady called Bonnie,
Whose feet were so wet and soggy,
When she sat down to eat,
She tripped over her feet
And now she stays at home with her doggie.

Danielle Ross (9)
Park Junior School

Friends

Friends are either good or bad.
If they're bad, they're obviously mad,
'Cause you're the bestest friends that were on Earth,
Maybe we were separated at birth.

Emma Pearson (9)
Park Junior School

A Giraffe Needs . . .

A patterned coat like paving stones
A tongue like Velcro
Long slender legs like stilts
And a neck as long as a pole.

Thomas Arnold (8)
Park Junior School

Bond

I have a friend called Bond
He was dizzy and fell in a pond
When he got up he was wet
He went to a shop to get a pet
And his hair is blonde.

Corey Starnes (9)
Park Junior School

Space

There is space
It is a wonderful place
There is no kind of race
It is just space
It is a wonderful place.

Jason Stephens (10)
Park Junior School

There Was A Boy

There was once a boy
Who ate his toy
But didn't tell
That he wasn't well
So he went ahoy!

Rebecca Lenton (10)
Park Junior School

THE BARMY BOYS OF ALEXANDRIA

There was a young man of Alexandria
Whose descendants got barmier and barmier
When his wife said it was so
He replied, 'Yes, I know,
But my grandson thinks he's in Narnia!'

Benjamin Robinson (9)
Park Junior School

PLACE TO PLACE

I want to go to the moon
I want to go real soon
Then I want to go to Mars
But I think I'll take a few chocolate bars
And then I want to go home
And last of all I want to go to the Dome.

Vaishali Vaghela (10)
Park Junior School

THE UNICORN

A coat as white as snow,
Its mane as soft as sheeps' wool,
Its head with a spike like an icicle,
Its feet like pebbles,
Its legs reach as high as the sky,
She's the beautiful unicorn.

Jade Smalley (9)
Park Junior School

JACKPOT

There was a man that won the jackpot
He was so happy he went over the moon
He was so delighted he chewed on a spoon
After that he smashed up the room
Before he won the jackpot it looked like doom.

Jamie King (8)
Park Junior School

ONE CHILD

One child weak
One child strong
One child short
One child long
One child cold
One child not.

Heetesh Chauhan (8)
Park Junior School

THE ELEPHANT

Skin like thick leather
Ears like big sheets of paper
Feet like big logs
Toes like pebbles.

Robert Henson (9)
Park Junior School

Birds, Birds

An owl will hoot
Maybe it shall toot
When it flies, it will swoop
You can teach it to fly through a hoop

A little bird called a finch
Will open, flinch
It's a common pet
So your mum should let

A mime bird you can teach to talk
It also has a very loud squawk
This bird is big and black
If it gets on your nerves don't give it a whack

A quail will only walk
It has a tweet not a squawk
Quails eggs are hard to find
So trying to get them will be a race against time.

Millie Brown (8)
Park Junior School

A Limerick About Maggie And Her Dog

There was a swordswoman called Maggie,
Her dog was enormous and shaggie,
When she took it for a walk
Her dog started to talk,
Then it went all waggie.

Dean Abbott (9)
Park Junior School

LOST PROPERTY

At school we have a lost property box.
An overflowing, overgrowing clothing dump!
And do you know, there are children
In our school walking around without . . .

9 pairs of shoes -
4 high heels and 5 boots
Without zips on them.

10 vests -
1 purple with green spots, 4 massive,
3 shrunk and 2 white with their sleeves pulled off.

2 pairs of socks -
1 pair stinking and the other rotten
Because they've been wrapped up all the time.

4 pairs of jeans -
1 without a button and 3 without the bottoms
As there's knives in the lost property box.

6 T-shirts -
3 with holes in and 3 without sleeves,
Oh no!

14 shirts -
10 all colours (yuk), 1 with spots and the other 3
With Mickey Mouse on (babyish).

Oh no, there are 45 things in the lost property box!

Tejal Joshi (8)
Park Junior School

The Old Man

There was an old man and he was always right
And one day he got in a fight.
His mind was very bright
And was as bright as a knight
And one night he got in a fright.

Lucy Byer (9)
Park Junior School

Kennings Monster

Human-eater
Flesh-licker
Tree-climber
Bug-catcher
Blood-sucker
Human-killer
Slow-eater
Bear-eater
Fire-eater
Kitten-lover
Angry-shouter
Wall-breaker
Mars-lover
Claw-scratcher
Door-smasher
Dam-destroyer
Knife-thrower
Brain-clinger
Big-dissector!

Luke Feakin (10)
St Edward's RC Primary School, Kettering

James Bond

James Bond is the best.
He is better than the rest.
With his gun he shoots them dead.
'The name's Bond, James Bond,' he said.
In his car he races around.
Trying not to make a sound.
All his gadgets blowing up.
(I'm surprised he hasn't given up).
Going round in a boat
In his black bullet-proof coat,
In bed with the girls
(Some with extremely long curls)
Always killing.
Blood spilling.

Thomas Goodfellow (11)
St Edward's RC Primary School, Kettering

McGrath

Good-starter
High-flyer
Corner-swooper
Neat-wooper
Wheelie-puller
Nac nac-performer
Race-winner
World-champ
Jeremy McGrath.

Graham Lee (11)
St Edward's RC Primary School, Kettering

My Kenning Poem About Me

Big-ears
Some-fears
Chip-eater
Deep-sleeper
Always-hungry
Quite-chubby
Loves-heights
Some-frights
Hates-pizza
Picky-eater
Squashes-bugs
Ugly-mug
Lots of freckles
Always-chuckles.

Liam Halloran (10)
St Edward's RC Primary School, Kettering

Beckham

Skilled-shooter
High-crosser
Fast-runner
Goal-scorer
Good-hacker
England-captain

David Beckham
Brooklyn's dad!

Andrew Law (11)
St Edward's RC Primary School, Kettering

JAMES BOND

Plant invader
Jack wader
Bomb dropper
Girl snogger
Mine exploder
Rifle loader
Watch stunner
Mad gunner
Boat racer
Car chaser
Inter com
Nuclear bomb
Dying day
PPK
Late night
Fist fight
Brief case
Toxic waste
Soldier shooter
Bank looter
Man scrambler
Casino gambler
Computer blaster
Gadget master
Door smasher
Villain basher
Valentine wager
Russian major
Runaway darting
Austin Martin.

Michael Pell (11)
St Edward's RC Primary School, Kettering

I READ A BOOK . . .

I read a book
About ships being tossed on the vicious seas
I read a book
About children dancing in the sun
I read a book
About autumn leaves floating silently down
I read a book
About a ghostly couple dancing at a phantom ball
I read a book
About a magical land where nothing goes wrong
I read a book
About the moon's reflection on a silver river
I read a book
From my imagination.

Gabriella DeMatteis (10)
St Edward's RC Primary School, Kettering

CRICKET

Fast-bowler
  Far-hitter
Great-catcher
  Field-keeper
Fine-fielder
  Wicket-hitter
Boundery-stopper
  Cricket-player!

Lloyd Mason (10)
St Edward's RC Primary School, Kettering

Crazy Candy

Liquorice-allsorts
    Toffee-apple
        Candy-stick
Lolly-stick
    Apples-sick
        Sour-lick
Sweet-teeth
    Big-shop
        Sweet-shop
Pineapple-cube
    Cola-cube
        Mr-Candy
Tiger-tongue
    Taz-bar
        Freddo-bar
Lacy-stick
    Dark-choc
        White-choc
Choco-holic
    Crazy-candy.

Aaron Heera (10)
St Edward's RC Primary School, Kettering

The River

The river flows down the hill
It shines brightly when the sky is blue
And glistens when the moon is out
You can see the stars
Glittering in the silver waves.

Amy Byrne (11)
St Edward's RC Primary School, Kettering

FOOTBALL CRAZY ALPHABET

A is for Arsenal, the best team in the world.
B is for Bergkamp, brilliant crosser.
C is for captain, the team's decider.
D is for defenders, who defend the attackers.
E is for excellent finisher.
F is for forwards.
G is for goals, which decide who wins the game.
H is for Henry, the best striker in France.
I is for Ireland, who won the Masters Cup.
J is for Justin Jackson, who is Rushden and Diamonds
leading goal scorer.
K is for keeper, who saves most of the shots.
L is for losers, who are always upset.
M is for Man U, Arsenal's arch enemy.
N is for numbers, on the back of their shirts.
O is for over, the ball always goes over.
P is for penalty, which are mostly always scored.
Q is for QPR, who Arsenal beat in the FA Cup.
R is for ref, the boss of the game.
S is for striker, who scores most of the goals.
T is for trainer, who trains the team.
U is for United, who won the treble last year.
V is for verve, a curling ball.
W is for woodwork, someone always hits it.
X is for Xtra time.
Y is for yellow card, the ref's best friend.
Z if for Zinidine Zidane, voted 2nd best player in France.

Stephanie Donald (10)
St Edward's RC Primary School, Kettering

THE YUMMY ALPHABET

A is for an apple pie all sweet and hot
B is for boiled sweets, all the flavours I like
C is for candyfloss, to melt in your mouth
D is for Dairy Milk chocolate, eat it all at once
E is for eggs, Cadbury's Cream Eggs, how do you eat yours,
F is for fudges, chewy but nice
G is for Galaxy chocolate bars, out of this world!
H is Haribo, Star Mix is my favourite
I is for ice cream, ever so cold
J is for Jammie Dodgers, biscuit and jam
K is for KitKat, with wafer inside
L is for Lemon Sherbet, tangy on your tongue
M is for Mars bars, heaven in each bite
N is for Nik Naks, nice and spicy are best
O is for orange chocolate, it's not Terry's, it's mine!
P is for Penguin, have them as a snack
Q is for the quick time it takes to eat a sweet
R is for Rolo Cookies, oh so nice!
S is for Skittles, the rainbow sweets
T is for Time Out, eat it when you want
U is for unreasonable amount of chocolate I eat
V is for very nice Starburst chews
W is for Wonkalate, the new chocolate bar
X is for Xmas, when we eat loads of chocolate
Y is for yummy things to eat
Z is for zero seconds I'd eat this all in.

Nikki Pell (10)
St Edward's RC Primary School, Kettering

Ghosts

Swooping past you
Sending a shiver shooting down your spine
Rattling your brains
You hold your breath
It feels like daggers digging into your back
Making your flesh creep
It's inside you, you don't know what to do
You blood turns cold
You stand still, trying to move but you can't
It's holding you down
Your stomach turns and rumbles
Bang
You wake up, it's all a dream
Until . . . tomorrow night it will come again.

Laura Mead (11)
St Edward's RC Primary School, Kettering

Chinese Night

A glowing light shines
Flickering without any sound
Chinese lanterns glow.

Blossom falls on clouds
Oriental silent, China Town
The red sunset comes alive.

Kieran Haddock (10)
St Edward's RC Primary School, Kettering

My Family

My brother is an alien,
From outer, outer space,
He runs about screaming
With an evil glare on his face.

My mother is a monster,
She roars around the house,
She shouts at me to tidy up,
Oh! And to be as quiet as a mouse.

My dad is a lunatic,
But then so am I,
He snores and snores so loud,
People must hear him in the sky.

Me, I'm just perfect,
Nothing like my family,
I don't shout or scream,
I'm happy as I am, just being me.

Elsa Smith (10)
St Edward's RC Primary School, Kettering

Me

I like food
    I like TV
I like chocolate
    I like bed
I like music
    I like family
I like friends
    I like me.

Shannon McGill (10)
St Edward's RC Primary School, Kettering

MIDNIGHT MEETING

Such a place to go,
so secluded, so secret

A dusky shadow cast around
as the sound of chaos
and disorder inside

The midnight meeting
carries on and on and on
till the ole grandfather clock
strikes *one*!

Rebecca Sephton-Pike (10)
St Edward's RC Primary School, Kettering

THE RIVER

Flows between the rushes
It flickers in the moonlight
Flow the river, flow.

Oliver Machell (11)
St Edward's RC Primary School, Kettering

CATS

Cats in straggly lines
Scaring off his enemies
Pouncing on his prey
Eyes like bright yellow lemons
He aims, he pounces, he's gone!

Adriana McAlindon (10)
St Edward's RC Primary School, Kettering

Stray Dog In Winter

Through the enchanting snow-covered town
the snow drops on his nose
but that is the least of his worries.
Just then he heard a sound,
it was raining.
His eyes looked as if he was crying.
He had red drippy eyes.
His legs all flea bitten
and its swollen pink tail
and rough leathery paws,
not to mention his long crooked ears.
Within a few days
picked up off of the street
being saved from death's door,
he has an owner once more.

Ellenagh Fisher (9)
St Patrick's RC Primary School, Corby

My Voyage To The Stars

I closed my eyes
and then began to imagine
I was dancing about
on a billion stars.
When I stood on a star
it started shining.
When every star was twinkling,
my voyage got better and better.

I opened my eyes
and heard a voice shout,
'Get out of bed!'

Gemma Carey (9)
St Patrick's RC Primary School, Corby

Flickering Flames

Flickering flames
licking, flicking
lacking, slacking
popping chopping.
The heat burning
bright heat of flames,
burning high with the glow.
Fantastic, even exciting.
Flickering flames
licking, flicking
lacking, slacking
popping, chopping.
The cool ashes
lay by my side.
Time to go.
The flickering flames
have ended.

Thomas Eaton (11)
St Thomas More RC Primary School, Kettering

Loads Of Money

I would like lots of money
It would be nice to win a tonne of it
Lottery, quizzes or the pools
I must obey all the rules
Buy a mansion, buy a car
Go on holiday to afar
Live by the sea and the sun
Life would be so much fun
I would buy myself a football team
And make sure I was never mean.

Jack Snype (10)
St Thomas More RC Primary School, Kettering

DANGEROUS SERPENT VOYAGE

Up above the sparkling waves
A voyage was happening
I looked into the ocean deep
Wondering what could be below

With my subtle cutlass in my scabbard
A scornful man walked up to me
'Beneath these seas there lives a serpent
Waiting to kill his next victim.'

There we were drifting along
In our cabins we ate the grub
Did our death await us
Or would we see another day?

An unnatural out of this world wail occurred
It sounded like the dying cries of a lowly cat.

Outside there was a serpent
Looking fearless at the crew,
It whacked the ship with its tail
Through the strong zephyr not struggling at all.

I swiftly pulled out my silver cutlass
And struggled to move
But soon I got to the edge of the ship.

I hit the serpent several times in the eye
And in the head
Finally it died, smacking the water
And gently it sank to its death below.

Soon our voyage ended
And I was ever scared of the sea,
For I had seen a serpent
And it had tried to kill me.

Samuel McAuley (11)
St Thomas More RC Primary School, Kettering

War

You may think of heroic deeds and failure
But war is at home,
The distant wailing of the death-trap bombs,
Distress, glory, failure, pain,
You're the victim, you're the bait,
That is war.

But there is war also away,
Families split apart,
Death, the front line
Fighting, using their guns
Lice, mud, the ravenous bombs
Go only for you,
Your best friend lying dead next to you
That is war.

Peter Hirst (11)
St Thomas More RC Primary School, Kettering

To Be A Cloud

Some people might wonder
What it's like to be a cloud,
To be fluffy and light,
To watch the starry sky at night
And to watch the sun shining in the day.

Sometimes I just wish
I could be something else,
A fly on the wall or a bird in its nest
And to be something else
If just a simple blade of grass
Just to be something else but a cloud.

Gemma Burns (10)
St Thomas More RC Primary School, Kettering

My Trumpet

My trumpet
Looks like
Meandering golden pipes
Glistening in the light of the hot sun.
It feels like
A close friend playing a fun game
With me on a warm summer's day.
It sounds like
A long foghorn
Sounding in the darkness of the night
When I play legato
But when I play staccato
It sounds more like an excited woodpecker,
Pecking on the hard bark of an old giant
Redwood tree.
It has a bell like a brilliantly yellow trumpet
Of new spring daffodils just opened up
Into the bright sunlight of a new day.
That's why the trumpet is my kind
Of instrument.

Thomas Pelley (11)
St Thomas More RC Primary School, Kettering

Oak Trees

They have immense brown trunks,
a dwelling place for squirrels,
their leaves are great fun for the kids in autumn,
they have acorns for the squirrels to eat,
their branches are interminable, strong and sturdy.

James Portch (10)
St Thomas More RC Primary School, Kettering

DOWN IN THE JUNGLE

Down in the jungle
lies a scaly snake,
hissing for its food.
But when the tiger comes along,
it goes in a log to hide.
The tiger scares the chirpy parrots
and scares the cheeky orang-utans.
It frightens away all the animals
with its big and scary *roar!*
But when the tiger goes away,
the orang-utans swing from branch to branch
and the parrots start to sing again
and the snakes get their food,
eventually.
So in the deep dark jungle,
at night the roaring lions sleep
like the rest of the cheeky animals.
So it's silent, almost.

Angelina Pepper (10)
St Thomas More RC Primary School, Kettering

THE SCHOOL

As it stands, tall and vast,
Passers-by wonder
What secrets it may contain
What may occur
Within its lifeless corridors?

Will the headmaster crack his cane?
Will the teacher give out sums?
Shall the bully dish out pain?
When will the bell ring for break?

The shadows will loom
And dust will gather
The children are gone
As another school closes.

Charlie Aylott (11)
St Thomas More RC Primary School, Kettering

The Owl And The Pussycat

The owl and the pussycat travelled afar,
In an ugly, old, lime green van.
They stopped at a pub and ate some grub
And a kilo of caviar.
The owl glared up to the clouds above
and screeched to a large violin
'Oh ugly pussy! Oh pussy my love!
What a terrible pussy you are,
You are,
What a terrible pussy you are!'

Pussy screamed to the owl
'Oh you smell disgustingly foul!
Your aftershave smells like a gone off Milky Way.
Hey, hey! A gone off Milky Way!

You pretend to be posh in that ridiculous coat,
But instead of wine,
You drink cheap Coke
And you bought me some knitting needles,
Oh yes! You bought me some knitting needles.'

Pussy slapped the owl around the beak
And the following day he had a bruised cheek.
So then he did decide to give up on finding a bride.
Hey, hey! To give up on finding a bride!

Hannah Glennon (10)
St Thomas More RC Primary School, Kettering

Slithering Sand Snake

Slithering in the sizzling desert
The sand snake came over the sandy hills
Looking for shade.
It found a cool, calm, comfortable place to rest,
It was a plant with a different snake in it.
The snake was hissing like a frying pan
    at the sand snake and attacked.

The sand snake had nowhere to go
When it saw a desert tree and cooled underneath it.
The sand snake looked back into the atmosphere
And saw some water,
It swiftly slithered to the water to have a drink.
After it returned, it slithered back to its
Comfortable home.

Stefan Pask (11)
St Thomas More RC Primary School, Kettering

The Sea

The sea, like a big blue silk sheet,
Laid along the beach,
Shining in the sunlight.
Fish in another world under the surface,
Swimming along peacefully,
Dolphins hunting silently,
Boats are sailing out to sea,
Floating on the waves,
Children playing in the water,
Happily splashing away.

Lauren Mitchell (10)
St Thomas More RC Primary School, Kettering

'Sony' A Game

There are lots of different PlayStation games,
in different boxes with different names,
in racing car games you get demolition,
with Tana on his secret missions.
In Spyro the Dragon you must collect all the loot
and smash all the boxes in Crash Bandicoot.
The evil is resident in Racoon City,
the last game I rented was rubbish which was a pity,
but the game I like out of all the rest,
Driver Two beats all the rest.

Sam Hall (10)
St Thomas More RC Primary School, Kettering

Backward Poem

I morning up in the woke
and breakfast my eat.
then I teeth my brush
and face my wash.
I'll changed get then
and bag out my sort.
The boring is quite journey,
so we radio to the listen.
My mum drop me hill
at the top of the off.
That my morning
helps boring.

Kyle Price (11)
St Thomas More RC Primary School, Kettering

MY SMALL FRIEND AND I

I've got an immensely minute friend,
We get in so much trouble.
We go out on many exotic adventures,
He's always by my side.

On Monday we strolled through an emerald jungle
We heard noises like a mummy monster
Coming in to find a baby monster
Pulling a very silly face.
But we were there for each other
Soon the noises died away.

On Tuesday we found a dangerous dragon,
He was scared when *we* pulled silly faces,
So he took us on a dragon ride
Over lots of cool places.

On Wednesday we found a monster
As big as a bubbling volcano.
He chased us to the river
Where we found a rickety boat with no row
But we didn't care, we were set to go.

On Thursday we clambered over and through
A frightening forest,
Creepers creeping up your spine onto your head.

On Friday we just stayed in bed,
I gave a little sigh, how wonderful it is
To have my small friend
And I.

Elizabeth Stevenson (11)
St Thomas More RC Primary School, Kettering

THE TOILET SONG

Swish, swash, swish,
swish, swash, gurgle,
gurgle, lick, lap, lick, lick,
lap, slurp, burp, splurt,
splish,
splash,
splat, water rushing,
splat, splish
splitter splatter
plop
this is how
the toilet goes.

Karis Lynch (10)
St Thomas More RC Primary School, Kettering

NOT A LOT ALLOTMENT

My allotment is bare
I wish I had my granny's,
she has a pond which
has twenty-five golden fish in it,
she has a pear tree
which has the best pears,
she has a rose patch
which has roses that smell
like honey,
she has a greenhouse
which grows the finest tomatoes.
My granny has everything
I wish I had my granny's allotment.

Faun Gower (10)
St Thomas More RC Primary School, Kettering

After Dark

Creepy noises at night,
Footsteps in the passageway,
Shadows on the wall,
Ghouls,
Spirits,
I'm afraid to shut my eyes.
Spooky howls,
Creaky noises from the door.

Doors creak open,
They're coming,
Hide under your bedclothes,
Don't look out,
Flashlights,
Death, hell,
They're coming to get me,
Helppp.

Morning
I adore morning
The sweet smell of freedom.

Kerry Harrison (11)
St Thomas More RC Primary School, Kettering

Down The Waterfall

Clear and blue the water's colour,
My life seems to get much duller.
Down I go, my hopes all fade,
Splashing like a tidal wave,
Until I see my true reflection,
Down the waterfall is my protection.

Shannon Elliott (11)
Warwick Primary School

FIREWORKS NIGHT

F ireworks, fireworks oh so wonderful fireworks,
I 'm having so much fun because we're having fireworks;
R ockets, disco lights, diamond showers and loads more,
E choing, boom, bang-a-boom, zooming, spreading all over,
W e're having so much fun.
O h oh, oh wondrous fireworks,
R ich colours, bright colours, fancy colours,
K eep away oh yes, oh yes, oh yes, keep away!
S uper sizzling fireworks, super flashing fireworks.

N ow look, here come some more fireworks,
I t's starting to get dark really fast,
G uess what comes next, team rocket, blast off,
H igh above the sky, look at all the colours, *bang,*
T ime to say goodbye till next year.

Sabrina Gemmell (10)
Warwick Primary School

THE ROSE

How art thou rose
As the doors of hatred close?
As the rose grows
And as the wind of love blows.
The light of darkness fades
As the light of children steps
Out of the shade.
The key is to love not to lose,
Before I go back to my cruise.
Remember, never shall the
Doors of love ever die.

Danielle Murdin (10)
Warwick Primary School

Winter

Outside the window I can see
The snow looking up at me.

His gleaming face looking back,
A white freshness he does not lack.

I wish I could go out to play,
But I have to wait for another day.

Snow like foam outside my house,
The wind is blowing as quiet as a mouse.

Trees outside bleak and bare,
Back at me they watch and stare.

The land outside, stiff with frost,
The snowman outside looks alone and lost.

Hannah Slough (10)
Warwick Primary School

Cats

Some cats are very fat,
They're always asleep on their little mat.
They are very, very furry
And cats like a bit of curry.
Some eat their cat food
And get in a mood.
Some are black and white
And their collars are tight.
when they see someone in sight,
They quickly look and
Run away if they might.

Rosey Kaur Sandhu (10)
Warwick Primary School

Bye Bye Summer, Hello Winter

Oh winter's here once again,
Summer hasn't been that bad,
Remember going to the lake
Who got pushed in?
Dad!

Remember going to Wicksteed Park,
I got a toy shark.
Mum was looking for us at 9pm
It wasn't even dark.

Now winter's here once again,
Wind, rain, snow,
Summer, summer, you're so nice,
Please don't go.

Chloe Brathwaite (9)
Warwick Primary School

Snow Is Fun

The snow is like a cold party of fun
When it comes you go off and run
You play in it, jump in it and other things
When the snow comes we are the snow kings
'Oh help, oh help!' The snowman calls
Which is made of snowballs
'Please help me, here comes the sun
For me there's no more fun.'
Oh look over there, there's a robin that sings
It flaps its feathered wings.
'Wait for me,' the robin calls
As they all fly over the walls.

Gemma Rogers (10)
Warwick Primary School

PARENTS SAY

Parents say this,
Parents say that,
Here are some parents' nags!

Do your bed,
Clean your room,
Eat up your bread,
Mop up with the broom.

Feed the fishes,
Clean the rat,
Do the dishes,
Don't forget about the cat.

What's the time,
Let's go to town,
Get some lime
And stop acting like a clown.

Do this,
Do that,
Can't I have some peace at last.

Sumita Mistry (10)
Warwick Primary School

MY FRIENDS

My name is Emma,
I live in a shoe.
My friends all like me
And I like them too!

One of them's Cally,
She's ever so small.
The other one's Gemma,
She's quite tall.

The others are:
Shannon, Hayley and gang.
We were all in the choir,
That's where we all sang.

Well, that sums it up,
They're all my friends.
I have no secrets,
I have no dead ends.

Emma Manning (10)
Warwick Primary School

Snow Is A . . .

The snow is an icicle,
Crisp and frozen.
It is a fluffy, white powder,
Just like flour.

The snow is a silent breeze,
Cold and frosty.
It is a white paint,
Laying softly.

The snow is a whistle
In the wind.
It is a howling wolf,
Howling in the sky.

The snow is an ice cream,
Melting in the sun.
It is a cloud, laying down.

Claire Smith (11)
Warwick Primary School

Me

I am a little idiot
As everyone now knows.
I have no senses of humour,
No arms, no feet, no nose.
Some people think they are mad
When they talk to their plants,
But I don't really care if they scream,
Sing or dance.
But when it comes to Christmas Day
They say it is too much to pay,
So why don't we scrap Christmas
And have Easter Day.
That's all I have to say, folks.
Good luck, goodbye and good day.

Jade Reid (11)
Warwick Primary School

Poetry

P is for poetic,
O is for okay,
E is for extreme,
T is for tried,
R is for rhyming,
Y is for yahoo.

Perfect, Okay, Extreme, Tried,
Rhyming and Yahoo
All make good poetry.

George Massingham (10)
Warwick Primary School

The Hamster Song

Neither goo nor slime have I,
But I patter on all four feet
And I have
Fun, fun, fun!

Neither toys nor sweets have I,
But I eat most of the day
And I have
Fun, fun, fun!

I master every little step,
For I snore, sleep and play
And I have
Fun, fun, fun!

Jodie Farnham (11)
Warwick Primary School

As Time Goes By

As I look out of my window
And watch the world go by,
I sit and think
Of my future
And I wonder why?
It's getting me in a muddle,
It's making me confused,
It's making my brain hurt!
So I'll leave it till tomorrow.
So it's tomorrow,
I'm still confused.
I can't think straight.
What can I do?

Cally Britten (11)
Warwick Primary School

MEMORIES

Time is lies,
Time is wonder,
Time is sunshine,
Time is thunder.

Time is happy,
Time is dim,
Time is fat,
Time is slim.

Time to lose,
Time to keep,
Time to waken,
Time to sleep.

I'll never forget
Any favour or crime
'Cos memories are all
That keeps time!

Hannah Szymanski (10)
Warwick Primary School

STARS AND THINGS

The sun is hot
The moon is cold
The stars are bright
The sky is bold
And all I do
Is wonder why
Stars and things live up so high!

Natalie Couchman (11)
Warwick Primary School

Nothing But Planets

I am a kite stuck in this strange place,
Somebody let go of me,
Now I'm here in space,
I'm lost for all eternity.

It's an unlit magical place sparkling with stars,
Planets whirling, swirling, spinning,
Help! There's no people. No water. No cars,
Nothing but planets in darkness, a never-ending flow of air.

I'm feeling kind of scared and very, very lost,
It's a strange magical dream waiting to be seen,
These planets must think I'm strange,
But they would have to come where I've been.

How did I get here? I'm stuck,
I don't want to die,
How planets are made, I haven't got a clue,
All I am is a little kite spy.

Victoria Watts (9)
Whitefriars Junior School

My Journey To Saturn

I'm an astronaut
I'm travelling through space
My journey is to Saturn
Will I get there if I race?
I climb into my spaceship
The stars are flashing by
My cousin is right beside me
He keeps saying, 'My, oh my!'

Timothy Ulyatt (10)
Whitefriars Junior School

Days From The Past

My name is Rebecca
I'm in 2040,
It was all a dream.

One night when I was fast asleep
I fell into the past
I twirled and swirled everywhere,
Until I landed,
Bang!
Dizzy and confused
I wondered where I was,
Was it all a dream?

Smell the factories smoke and fire,
Almost taste the appetising bread from the bakers,
Feel the touch of the people's clothes,
Hear the children screaming,
Then it fell into place,
I was in a lively, bustling London street
In Victorian times,
Could it have been a dream?

I wandered into a factory
And found a little girl,
We made friends at once,
She told me she was a dunce,
As if she was in a dream.

Me and the girl, we strolled down the street,
We talked and chatted about our lives,
It was nothing like our teacher told us!
A horse and carriage trotted by, a rich boy smirked at us,
He looked as smug as a cat with the cream,
My friend just froze and gritted her teeth,
It felt like a dream.

Soon after that I went forwards in time to modern days,
I had fun and games 'til my adulthood,
But one night, time repeated itself
And whizzed back to Queen Vicky's reign,
It felt real, but was it a dream?

To my surprise, this time I flew everywhere,
I swished and swashed and swooved,
Peering into the windows of a mansion,
I saw my friend playing with her children.
I peeped in a workhouse window,
Saw a person I was certain I'd seen before.
It was all a dream *or was it?*

Rebecca Rowley (10)
Whitefriars Junior School

THE FRIENDLESS SHOOTING STAR

I am a shooting star
As I light the sky,
The Earth is so far.

Every night when I shoot
I see a little boy,
I wonder what he's thinking about
When he's playing the flute.

I've been in the sky for millions of years,
Every night when I shoot I wish I had some friends,
When will my life end,
I hate being a star,
Would you?

Daniel Clarkson (9)
Whitefriars Junior School

SUN

I am the biggest planet up here
The one who gives you light
I'm red and yellow with shreds of orange
But also I am so bright

I look at all the other planets
And see them twinkling to each other
I don't talk to anyone
But I know I'm like their mother

I wish I could move about
And spin round and round
Also go and explore
What is on the ground

I think about how I got up here
And when I'm going to die
Shimmering and shining
In the dark so high?

Hayley Channell (10)
Whitefriars Junior School

THE TRAVELLING STAR

I am a star,
I am a bright shining star,
I travel through the galaxies
I fly at supersonic speed
My twinkling family are all around me
So I am never lonely.

I find planets,
I find huge planets,
Like Mars, Jupiter and Earth
But I know you know this star well
It is your light giver, yes, the sun.

I've travelled far,
I've travelled further than man,
The Earth is wonderful
Bright green and blue
Mars is a relaxing dull red.

Jason Huckle (10)
Whitefriars Junior School

I Am A Grandfather Clock

I am a grandfather clock,
My wood is battered
And my glass door is smashed and smeared,
I am an old grandfather clock all shattered.

I am a grandfather clock,
I go back in time to the factory
Where I was made,
To the year 1893.

I am a grandfather clock,
I dream about the mines
And I think about poor children
As I go back in time.

I am a grandfather clock,
My friends are the halls
Where I stand and tick,
Against cold, bumpy walls.

I am a grandfather clock,
When will I die?
Will I ever stop?
I stand still and sigh.

Zoe Brealey (9)
Whitefriars Junior School

A VICTORIAN CHILD

My task is to be a maiden.
To work for rich families.
I work for money to buy some honey.
Everyday I peer out of my window,
To find children being whipped.

The coal mines are dirty, dusty and dangerous.
In the factories people feel terrified, horrified.

I fancy to be prosperous, me and my family
But I doubt I ever can be.
A long skirt for me!
A shirt, will it suit me?
I would be rich just like them!

Then I met a boy
I had never seen before.
Then a man and woman and a daughter.
This must be a rich family.
I shivered and ran home.
I will never see that family again.

Lucy Jekyll (9)
Whitefriars Junior School

I AM A STAR

I am a star
I wander through space
Exploring the galaxies
Listening at my own pace.

I am a star
I smell Earth's luscious water
I smell sun's blazing fire
I treat space as my daughter.

I am a star
I feel terrorised near Earth
And the same with sun
I felt like this since my birth.

I am a star
I wonder how I got here
I wish I could venture to Earth
Did I come from far or near?

Georgiana Goss (9)
Whitefriars Junior School

THE LONELY STAR

I am a star,
I float round the moon,
It takes a long time
But I get round it soon.

I wonder if my life will ever end,
I've been up there for millions of years,
I am lonely, without any friends,
I cry out my tears.

I wish I had some friends,
I am so scared,
I twinkle and shine
But I don't know if anyone cared.

I am so lonely,
Can I get to Earth?
Or must I travel the galaxy
Where I had my birth?

Jade Reece (10)
Whitefriars Junior School

My Day As A Victorian

Oh, I don't like it here!
They all eat deer.
That's if you're rich,
Not if you're poor.

I like being rich!
You get all the yummy, yummy food
And all the toys
And you don't have to work.

Do I like being poor
With no food or toys?
You *have to work . . .*
In coal mines or up chimneys.
No!
I don't like being poor.

I don't like going to school!
You get beaten to death
With the cane,
When you're a pain.
You have to repeat over and over again
And the drill is my *worst*!

I met the Queen;
Queen Victoria.
I brought back her ring
But she said I stole it!

I'd rather be home in 2001!

Brett Clembintson (10)
Whitefriars Junior School

I Had A Dream Last Night

I had a dream last night,
A little girl appearing,
She was very rich,
But she was fearing.

I had a dream last night,
A little boy was crying,
He was very poor,
And he was sighing.

I had a dream last night,
I was going back in time,
I saw all the poor children,
But they didn't look fine.

I had a dream last night,
I was going back in time,
I felt all alone and lonely,
Like poor children time to time.

I had a dream last night,
A little girl appearing,
She was very rich,
But she was fearing.

Who put them there?
Who are they?
Why in my dream?
Who can say?

Kayleigh Malins (10)
Whitefriars Junior School

ONE IN A MILLION

I twinkle and sparkle
I gleam and glitter
But up in the sky
I'm just a flicker.

I want to dazzle far and near
In the light and in the clear
But unfortunately stars are rife
I live unnoticed
And that's my life.

One in a million
That's me,
I want to be special
But I'm not even a dot you can see.

The North Star is noticed
Why not me?
Perhaps if I went there
I could be free.

Stars, meteorites and even the moon
Comets flashing past
As if racing each other
Trying not to be last.

Something's happening to me
I keep spluttering and fizzing
While I'm shooting through space
Zooming and whizzing.

I have reached my destiny
But I have been altered on my trip
I think I am dying
R.I.P.

Kayleigh Betterton (10)
Whitefriars Junior School

THE BATTLE OF THE PLANETS

It was a day off
Out here in space
Dark and mystical
A horrible place.

I'll tell you the facts
Of the horrible battle
Of the planets do their wish
And I'll warn you
This will make your head rattle

One day it was a normal and peaceful
Day out in space
When all of a sudden they started to frown
And they were pulling an appalling face.

They started to huff and puff
And crash and bash
Like a monstrous bull
Destroyed in a flash.

Pluto spoke in a thunderous voice
I'll freeze you all
I will be the king of space
And be strong and tall.

They started to trip and kick
And thump and bump
Destroying themselves
With all their fury.

And suddenly everything stopped
In a blaze of light
They were disabled and paralysed
And not able to fight.

Grant Chambers (10)
Whitefriars Junior School

TWINKLING STAR

I am a little star
My name is Sparkle
I wonder how I got here
Maybe someone shot me up here
I can see a huge sun
Just waiting for me.

I'm a little star
I don't know how I got here
I feel really scared with no one around here
I just wish I had someone to talk to.

I can hear little sparkles of fire
Flashing right past me.
I feel really lonely because I have no friends
All of the other stars have bright, twinkly sparks.

I'm a little star
I don't know how I got here
I feel really scared with no one around here
I just wish I had someone to talk to.

Sarah Allison (9)
Whitefriars Junior School

A JOURNEY TO SPACE

Bolting off into space,
We were going so fast that it was like in a race,
We were travelling right above,
The planets are what I love.

I see fantastic shooting stars,
I hear the comets fly around Mars,
I see Mercury which is nearest to the Sun,
But while I'm up in space I miss my mum.

It feels so silent up there,
It is like nobody cares,
Space is as black as coal,
Space gets to my brain and my soul.

I land, tumbling down on the Earth,
It feels weird and bouncy on turf
I'm glad to see night and day.
I wish I could up and away.

Holly Smith (10)
Whitefriars Junior School

A Victorian Childhood

I am Bobby.
I am a chimney sweeper.
I'm mucky because I go up chimneys
When they are still too hot.
So silent and dark.

Outside is snow and wind
Mist and fog
People dying and starving.

I'm thinking, will I soon die?
In the factory I am so scared.
I stole something from the factory;
Coal and some string.

Will I die up a chimney?
To be left there to rot?
I do not like Victorian life.

Michael Kura (9)
Whitefriars Junior School

ROCKY ROCKET

I am Rocky Rocket!
I look like a rocket of course!
I am wicked red on my front.
But all electrical inside!

I am Rocky Rocket!
I am always delighted when I zoom off,
But I normally feel sick in outer space!
My problem is I don't know the way to Saturn,
So I have a chat with the moon.

I am Rocky Rocket!
The moon tells me to go left,
So I could get to Saturn,
Finally I reach it, and have a little chat,
We chat about the other planets to see if they have life!

I am Rocky Rocket!
Now it is time to go,
I have to blast off back to Earth,
I think I'll never see Saturn again,
I just want to live in Saturn!

I am Rocky Rocket!

Bradley Bunce (9)
Whitefriars Junior School

JOURNEY TO SPACE

Press start, go to space like a dart,
Flying through space, seeing meteors go past,
Dodging them like a cheetah fast.

Stop here, see the stars,
Also look at great big Mars,
There's the aliens in their motor cars.

Unbuckle, float around,
You can hear all different sounds,
We are nowhere to be found.

Sophie Ayres (10)
Whitefriars Junior School

VOYAGER 3

Floating is a spacecraft
On a voyage through space
In a spacecraft named Voyager III
They're going in a ship that's ace!

They're heading for Pluto
The planet that's freezing cold
From the ship they can view the moon
The craters startle because they're black and bold

The crew see an unusual thing
So they check under the bonnet
There are no faults . . .
So what they've seen is definitely a comet!

Panic, panic, panic around
There's a chance they'll die
Calm, calm, calm everyone
Pray you don't have to say goodbye.

It's getting closer
There will be a big bang
Get down, remember the prayers you sang
It's coming, now it's all over
Duck now, here it comes . . .
Bang!

Joseph Passby (10)
Whitefriars Junior School

I Am The Moon

I live in space
I'm very white
I come out at night
And I'm a bright light

I am the moon
My place is space
I spin around the Earth
Having a great race.

All I see is blobs of gold
Racing around in the ground
I think it is pounds in the grounds
What race all around.

I am the moon
My place is space
I spin around the Earth
Having a great race.

There is a mystery
In deep dark space
It is stars
Always race.

I am the moon
My place is space
I spin around the Earth
Having a great race.

Daniel Pullen (10)
Whitefriars Junior School

BLAST INTO SPACE

Blast into space
Blast into space
Yes here we go
Yes here we go
Amazing pace
Amazing pace
Not going slow
Not going slow

Sparkling bright stars
Sparkling bright stars
Planets all around
Planets all around
Saturn, Venus, Jupiter and Mars
Saturn, Venus, Jupiter and mars
Nothing makes a sound
Nothing makes a sound

Blast back home
Blast back home
I'm zooming past
I'm zooming past
I'm all alone
I'm all alone
I'm home at last
I'm home at last.

Adele Pinnock (10)
Whitefriars Junior School

The Journey Through Space

I am an astronaut
I'm getting in my rocket
The countdown has begun

I am now in space
I am in a wondrous place
There's a warning in the sky
That a planet is going to blow up
It will glide and glide until it can fly

The planet misses
So we can go home
I have enjoyed my day
In the middle of May.

Chantelle Gibson (10)
Whitefriars Junior School

Nothing There

It was finally May,
the very big day,
the day of the launch.

The very next day,
they were set away,
leaving no trace.

When they were there,
they were in despair,
finding nothing there.

They landed the spaceship,
it happened in a bang,
like a caught boomerang.

Harry Hiams (9)
Whitefriars Junior School

JOURNEY TO MARS

10 seconds until we go,
Rumble, rumble!
Where we'll land I don't know,
Rumble, rumble!

Here we go, we're off at last,
Boom, boom!
We're going so quick, no time has passed,
Boom, boom!

Nearly there, we'll be there soon,
Shudder, shudder!
Oh no, we're on the moon,
Shudder, shudder!

Better not get out,
Shiver, shiver!
It might not be safe to walk about,
Shiver, shiver!

I hope the engine is not too bad,
Tremble, tremble!
When I get home, I'll be glad,
Tremble, tremble!

Thank goodness it's all right,
Phew, phew!
Wow, what a sight
Phew, phew!

So my journey to Mars went wrong,
Oh dear, oh dear!
I'm glad I wasn't there for long,
Oh dear, oh dear!

Lily Capewell (9)
Whitefriars Junior School

Dream Angel Of Neptune

Off I go from cloud number nine
I am the dream angel of Neptune
As my wings dance through the sky
I lash out a dream from my satchel

I deliver dreams from Elac to Zoroka
But yet I do not mind when
The hurricane winds brush against my feathers
As I feel like a laser,
I feel like a wild animal
Dashing through the air.

I see stars,
Where the nice people live
I see chilling ice and gentle water
And the eight deserted moons
Magical animals and birds
Sleeping in the gloom.

Although I question myself,
About what it would be like to be normal
And the nightmare devil
Receives his nightmares from
Letting out my question
Of why am I here,
Why is anything here.

Back I go through the stars
To the universe with no Venus or Mars
Flying through the entrance I go
To the land without any snow
That's the one cloud number nine
There's the house, the house so fine
The house I live in all the time
That's the one cloud number nine.

Adam Newell (9)
Whitefriars Junior School

The Minute Little Star

I'm a minute little star blazing in the sky
I stare down at the Earth from way up high
A neglected little star billions of miles away
I make out Mars and Jupiter far, far away.

I long to be with other stars
Hovering over Jupiter and Mars
I recognise the other stars as glittery disco balls
Shining day and night.

Will I ever be a shooting star
Shooting over Mars?
Shall I be like this forever?
And shall I ever die?

I can see shooting stars like a rising rainbow
I wish I could be one. They say I might be able
But I still don't know if they're correct
Still waiting, just hope they're right.

Cathy Collins (9)
Whitefriars Junior School

THE JOURNEY TO JUPITER

I am a boy named Matthew,
Who wants to travel through space.
I want to land on a planet,
In such a special place

I've got to get ready quickly,
My journey is going to start
I'm nearly ready, yes I am,
I've got my space suit, every part.

Now I have gone in my spaceship,
I have started my journey.
I have just landed.
What's this I see?

They look like aliens blowing wind,
Did I just say blowing wind?
Aliens don't blow wind,
Wish I didn't get thrown or binned.

The aliens are doing the weirdest stare,
The kind that makes you want to run,
The aliens seem infuriated
Maybe it's the thought of being far away from the sun.

The angry aliens have a bomb,
What on earth for?
Or should that be what on Jupiter?
Oh this is such a bore.

The aliens have just thrown the bomb,
It's on direct hit for my spaceship,
I'd better cover my ears,
I wish I had the whip.

I suddenly hear the big boom!
I really wish I was home.
But how will I get there?
I promised to give my dog a bone.

Suddenly I hear a *ping*!
I strangely see my house
And a fairy with a wand,
Then I saw a cat chasing a mouse.

Now I'm home,
By the weirdest travel
Now that I am at home sweet home
I'm glad I see the outside gravel.

Matthew Fortescue (10)
Whitefriars Junior School

My Journey

I'm Kia,
A flower seller,
I'm very mucky
From the mud.
Every day when
I'm out it's
Cold and wet.

There's a dream
I always have,
I wonder if
It's real,
I wish it were.

I might die soon,
I'm frightened.

Briana Groom (9)
Whitefriars Junior School

JOURNEY OF A METEOR

I am a meteor,
Rocketing through space!
I race through the universe,
Without leaving a trace!

I shoot past Venus,
I rocket past Mars!
I cruise my way past Jupiter
And separate the stars!

I wish and wish that I could get bigger,
But in space I keep sailing through,
Then the funny thing I found
My wish had plainly come true!

Then I decide to hit planet Earth!
It's better than floating out here,
But as soon as I get much too close,
I burn up in Earth's atmosphere!

Victoria Pierce (9)
Whitefriars Junior School

THE EARTH, SUN AND MOON

One afternoon,
The Earth, sun and moon
Went for a walk
But none of them would talk.

The Earth went back to his house
And felt as tired as a tiny little mouse,
Then the moon went to bed
Felt as tired as his old uncle Fred.

The sun light,
Hadn't slept all night,
But then he wondered,
He wondered.

Then one day
The sun came to say
I want a friend
Until the very, very end.

Denae McGowan (10)
Whitefriars Junior School

RACE TO SPACE

Who will win the race to space?
Ready, steady, go, we start,
We shoot off like a dart
Who will win the race to space?

Who will win the race to space?
Shooting, whizzing all around,
I'm so high, I can't see the ground
Who will win the race to space?

Who will win the race to space?
We're so fast, they're so slow
In the sky you sure do glow
Who will win the race to space?

We have won the race to space,
We have luckily come first.
It was because the other rocket burst,
We have won the race to space.

Amy Perry (10)
Whitefriars Junior School

Travelling Back In Time

When will someone go back in time,
For everyone's dream will come true,
But when someone finally gets there,
Everyone will come along too,
When will someone go back in time.

When will someone go back in time,
Suddenly I ran over a lump,
Before I knew where I was
I was in Victorian times.

Finally someone went back in time
It was dirty, scary and smelly,
For finally someone had got there
But they didn't have a telly.

Finally someone went back in time,
But suddenly went over a lump
Before I knew where I was,
I was back to my normal time.

Rebekah Yates (9)
Whitefriars Junior School

Manic Mars!

I zoomed into space
And landed on Mars,
I met some aliens
Driving red cars!

It's dark, it's cold,
I'm brave, I'm bold,
I want to go home now,
Mummy, Mummy,
I have a worry in my hungry tummy.

I get back in and
Start 'er up and count 1,2,3,
I zoom back home
And have a great big cup of tea.

Natalie Cheetham (10)
Whitefriars Junior School

JOURNEY TO THE MOON

Here I am yet again,
About to go into space yet again
Time to blast off
5, 4, 3, 2, 1,
We have lift-off.
Here we are in space
We can see the Earth, all of it.
Wow, we're nearly there.
Bang! Wallop! Crash!
Where are we.
We're not there.
What are they?
Wow! We're lost in space.
What planet is this?
We don't know.
What plant is that?
We don't know.
We're lost in deep space
No one will find us
I'm scared.
Oh my, oh my,
We're lost . . .
Just me and my dad.

Kyle Chapman (10)
Whitefriars Junior School

THE JOURNEY ON EARTH

Sitting in my spaceship
Waiting for the countdown
5,4,3,2,1
Time to blast off
And off we go.

Now I'm on my way
How long will I stay?
Something's going wrong
Why are we not landing on the moon?

We have gone off course
It is too soon
We need to land around here
How I wish it was the moon.

Thomas Downs (9)
Whitefriars Junior School

THE STUFFED ANIMAL

Once you were free
Free to swim in the river
But now you're in a glass box
Standing, standing still
Never to swim or breath again
You're just an ornament on the fireplace
Cold and silent.
With eyes that can't see
And a nose that can't smell
You're dead.
No longer part of this world.
You're dead.

Kristopher R Kilsby (9)
Windmill Primary Foundation School

My Dark Bedroom

It's dark in my bedroom.
I look around,
No one's there
I hear breathing in the corner of my room
I get cold and shaky
I hide under the cover and try to close my eyes
The breathing's getting louder.
I open my eyes
I see a shadow on the wall
I start shaking and shivering
I don't know what to do,
Who is it?
What do they want?
I look at the door
Someone's there.
It's only my mum
Standing at the door,
Which made the shadow on my wall.

Keeley Brinkhurst (10)
Windmill Primary Foundation School

The Stuffed Bird

You are hatched from an egg.
You are alive.
You are free.
But now you are on a shelf.
Dead and stuffed
You will never fly again.
You will never eat and sleep
All you will do is stand on a shelf
Never to feel the wind in your feathers again.

Michael Calders (10)
Windmill Primary Foundation School

THE EMPTY SKULL

You once had the life
But now you're still,
Cold bone, silent.
All around remains the spirit
You were once free
Now you're trapped inside the skull
Waiting to be freed.

You were once loud
But now you can only hear the wind and the rain
What are you?
Were you free?
Were you trapped by death?

The answers remain in the skull.
But no one dare go near it
For they say you will bring bad luck.
All that remains is the shadow of the skull.

Adam Rice (10)
Windmill Primary Foundation School

THE SKULL

Once I was free
Once I was a dog
I had fur
What have I got now?
I'll never move again
I'm not part of the world anymore.

Once I was fit
Once I was brave
What has become of me?
Cold thin bone
I sit motionless
Silent and cold

My eyes just stare, never to work again
I had fur
I had eyes
I have nothing now
Not even a bit of strength
What has become of me?

William Day (9)
Windmill Primary Foundation School

My Dark Bedroom

I am in my bedroom
It's more than dark
I can't see a thing
I am as frightened as anything
It feels like someone's in my bedroom
I hear deep breathing
There's a shiver all over me
My heart is beating fast
There are creaks on the floorboards
Now I'm scared
I'm hot
I'm sweating
I quickly grab hold of something
It feels like hairs sticking to my hand
Then I panic
I scream
I wish I hadn't done that
In the morning
I thought it was a nightmare
But there is hair on my hand
It isn't mine
Now I wonder if someone was really there.

Chanade Henderson (10)
Windmill Primary Foundation School

The Old Ruin

There in front of me stands a house
As I draw nearer the house grows bigger and bigger
I could probably touch it.

Now I'm so close I trip.
My fingertips go numb as I touch the leftover of the ruin
It crumbles and I jump back to dodge the falling rubble.
Is it safe to go in?

Out comes my torch as I step inside.
The wind howls and dust and grit falls on top of me.
I cough, I'm scared
The cough echoes all around me.

At the noise,
Rubble falls and covers the exit.
I shiver at the thought that I can't get out.
The only solution is to shout for help
But my throat is dry and the walls are weak.

Jennifer Turvey (9)
Windmill Primary Foundation School

The Ghostly Ruin

The old and ruined
Ghostly house of the 16th Century
That used to stand in the middle of nowhere.
Now lies on the floor.

Howls at night, scare the new village.
The crumbly rubble reveals the ghosts.
When you see the broken glass you see eyes.
Everybody cries, 'Move this house away'.

The mystery stays secret.
More than ever.
Everyone wants to know
What is the mystery?

Charlotte Firth (10)
Windmill Primary Foundation School

The Ruin

It's midnight and all is still.
I'm watching the ruin,
It's said to be haunted.
The outline of the ruin is clear
Owls are looking all around
I'm cold and frightened.

Why did I come?
Nobody would believe me if I did see a ghost
Why then am I waiting here for no reason?
Was it a dare?
Or did I decide to come?
Anyway I'm here and that's all that matters.

Wait, smoke is coming from the chimney
Is it a ghost cooking? Or not?
I shall find out,
No it was my imagination.
I'm going home to bed
Goodbye for now I shall be back.

I wake up the next day
Thinking about last night
Was it a dream or not?
I think and think about yesterday
What was I doing out there?

Sally Wright (10)
Windmill Primary Foundation School

The Ghostly Ruin

The ghostly ruins of a 16th Century house
Stand in a lonely wood in the middle of nowhere.

Crumbling walls covered in moss
Scary and ghostly
Windows like glaring, red eyes.

Howls and cries from the empty ruin
Mysteries are locked from the 16th Century
Feelings are locked from the 16th Century,
Things that will never be discovered.
Weeds are growing where floors once were
Where children used to play.

The house is now barb-wired
Animals running in the ruins of an old house
Ghosts roaming in walls and ruins
The ghosts of a family that used to live there.

Amy Jones (10)
Windmill Primary Foundation School

Grizzly Bear

Four big paws,
Stamping on the ground
Two pointed ears
Listening for sounds
Two staring eyes,
Looking for trouble
Roaming round the woods,
You better watch out
Big grizzly bears
Are zooming about.

Jayne Stewart (9)
Windmill Primary Foundation School

The Old Ruin

The ruin has no windows
Just stands there in the dark.
The door is half open
Waiting for someone to go in.

Shall I go in?
Or shall I not?
I know there's someone in there
No, I'll stand outside.

I am as quiet as a mouse
Unless someone hears me.
I might faint in a minute
In the old dark ruin.

I might hide behind a tree
But gravestones surround me.
I see a white person in the window.
Is she dead?
I run as far away as I can from the ruin!

Ashley Richards (10)
Windmill Primary Foundation School